Double Belonging

Interchurch Families
and Christian Unity

by
George Kilcourse

Paulist Press ♦ New York/Mahwah, N.J.

APPRECIATIONS
The Publisher gratefully acknowledges use of the following materials: Quotations from "Eucharistic Sharing from the Perspective of Roman Catholic Law," by James H. Provost, from *Food for the Journey* (Albuquerque, New Mexico: EDEO NADEO, 1985); and quotations from *Two Churches—One Love: Interchurch Marriage Between Protestants and Roman Catholics* (Dublin: APCK, 1977), reprinted with the permission of Professor Dr. A.I.C. Heron and the A.P.C.K. (The Association for Promoting Christian Knowledge).

Library of Congress Cataloging-in-Publication Data

Kilcourse, George, 1947–
    Double belonging : interchurch families and Christian unity / by George Kilcourse.
        p. cm.
    Includes bibliographical references and index.
    ISBN 0-8091-3292-3 (pbk.)
    1. Family—Religious life.   2. Marriage—Religious aspects—
Christianity.   3. Intermarriage.   4. Ecumenical movement.
I. Title.
BV4526.2.K54   1992
261.8′35843—dc20   91-28516
                                                                          CIP

Published by Paulist Press
997 Macarthur Boulevard
Mahwah, New Jersey 07430

Printed and bound in the
United States of America

Contents

To my mother and father,
Carol and George,
who first taught me
the love of Christ

Acknowledgments

This is a book I had no plans to write. Its parents are the interchurch couples whose experience and faith I have encountered at various workshops and talks which I offered around the country during the past four years. Their desire for a tool to provide a catalyst for more effective pastoral ministry to interchurch families persuaded and encouraged me to develop this study.

The first to be thanked for their vision and unfailing responses to my hunger for research materials are Ruth and Martin Reardon, and René Beaupère. During the past two decades, the British and French interchurch family movements were born and nurtured through their visionary lives and ministry. These pioneers have been generous beyond the telling with correspondence, patient dialogue, and the warmest of friendships.

During 1985 and 1986 the National Association of Diocesan Ecumenical Officers (NADEO) gave me free rein as Director of the Research and Development Committee to pursue the new frontier of interchurch families in the United States. I am especially grateful to John H. McDonnell and Ernest E. Falardeau, presidents of NADEO; committee members Ray Barton, Bob Dalton, Bert Mulroy, and Marge Nurnberg; as well as the national network of Roman Catholic ecumenical officers, for support, encouragement, and collaboration which eventuated in the 1987 NADEO booklet, *Ecumenical Marriage: An Orientation Booklet for Engaged Couples, Families, Pastoral Ministers, Religious Educators.*

I cannot think of interchurch families without a kaleidoscope of faces turning before my eyes. First are the couples and children themselves. I dare not begin to list them because inevitably many would be left out by my poor memory for names. What matters is the fact that they are the *human face* of ecumenism! But let me not neglect to express thanks to the leadership of our local interchurch couples in the Highlands Community Ministries group of Louisville: Rachelle and Mike Galvin, Mary Jane and Pete Glauber, Jenny and Jim Shircliff, and Marilu and Dade Luckett. And no persons in ministry have been more devoted or supportive of our endeavor than HCM's director, Stan Esterle, or Stanley A. Schmidt, my mentor in pastoral ecumenism, and Gregory Wingenbach, Director of the Kentuckiana Interfaith Community. The Louisville Southern Baptist–Roman Catholic Dialogue, and Kentuckiana Disciples of Christ–Roman Catholic Dialogue have both challenged and helped me in efforts to address the issues of this book.

Our national confederacy of local chapters of the American Association of Interchurch Families (AAIF, c/o Kentuckian Interfaith Community, 1115 South 4th Avenue, Louisville, KY 40203), while only three years old, speaks convincingly of the emergence of interchurch families as a gift to the churches. The important development of interchurch elements within existing marriage ministry organizations is reflected in the opportunities to audition some of the reflections in these pages at the 1989 National

Association of Diocesan Catholic Family Life Ministers (NACDFLM) convention, and to the 1990 National Engaged Encounter convention.

For the summer of 1985 I was awarded a research grant from Bellarmine College to develop a monograph on the pastoral and theological groundings of the English and French interchurch family models, which had begun in 1968. My thanks to Dean Thomas Greenfield and the grant committee for this important support, which eventuated in my article, "Ecumenical Marriage: Two Models for Church Unity," *Mid-Stream* 26 (1987) 189–214. I owe a special debt to my Bellarmine students in our "The Church in Renewal" classes. Their responsive engagement with the focal issue of interchurch marriage taught me much about the dynamics of teaching and learning theology. Most of all, I am encouraged that these intelligent, cheerful, and loving young people see themselves as the artisans of the ecumenical future, themselves candidates for interchurch marriage and family life.

The wonderful families I met at the international Association of Interchurch Family (AIF) conferences in Lingfield, England (1988) and Corrymeela, Northern Ireland (1990) gave me a perception of the interchurch family movement as truly the work of the Holy Spirit. The hospitality and faith of so many I met during these pilgrimages has touched me deeply, and given me energy to reflect upon their experiences with new hope.

In the midst of my many other plans and projects, it was Michael Downey who urged me to devote myself first to this book. He patiently helped me to discern its potential. He read various drafts of the manuscript and made many careful suggestions. Special thanks to him for being a more than helpful reader whose comments developed into a genuine dialogue about some of the theological issues of ecumenism, and a spirituality of marriage.

My gratitude goes to David Hargrove, a graduate student at the Southern Baptist Theological Seminary in Louisville, who patiently and carefully constructed this book's index.

Finally, I am indebted to my editor, Lawrence Boadt, who assisted me in developing the structure of the book, and encouraged me throughout the editorial process by direct, specific suggestions that have made this a better book.

1. The Phenomenon of Interchurch Marriage

Imagine a caravan of families arriving at a crossroad. A signpost, stacked with directional arrows, indicates that Anglicans take this road, Baptists take that highway, Roman Catholics follow another interchange, Presbyterians go straight ahead, and on and on through the list of denominations. The cars halt on the shoulder of the road, as families decipher the maze of routes. Each family is an *interchurch family:* the wife and husband each participates in his or her respective church, and to various degrees in one another's church; and each takes a conscientious and active role in the religious education of his or her children. The children find themselves at home in the church of either parent. When confronted with this signpost these interchurch families say, "No! We will not separate our families. We are staying together." And an aggravating question uncoils, "Now, where do we go?"

The engineers who design the signs are summoned to the scene by anxious state police troopers who are growing concerned over the now lengthy caravan, stalled on the shoulder of the interstate. The families patiently explain their dilemma. The children laugh because they find the directions impossible. Against the background din of passing traffic, the engineers listen to the interchurch families' story. They look again at the totem-pole of signs, this time with surprised eyes.

Interchurch marriages are a particular kind of "mixed marriage." We readily use the label "mixed marriage" to categorize couples who marry someone outside their own denomination, or even outside their own faith. For generations now Roman Catholics have generically dubbed the marriage of a Catholic to a "non-Catholic" as a "mixed marriage." That could include an unlimited variety: Catholic-Jewish, Catholic-Baptist, Catholic-Lutheran, Catholic-Buddhist, Catholic-atheist, Catholic-Jehovah's Witness, etc. To call these "ecumenical marriages" gives a positive connotation, but equally misnames the uniqueness of our families at the crossroad. An interchurch marriage differs because (1) it joins in marriage two baptized Christians from different traditions, (2) each spouse participates actively in her or his particular church, and to various degrees in one another's church, and (3) each spouse takes an active, conscientious role in the religious education of his or her children. In reality, interchurch marriages are a smaller (albeit significant) category within the larger pool of mixed marriages. Interchurch marriages encompass those Christian spouses from separated churches, both of whom refuse to "drop out" of their church, or to abdicate parental responsibility for their children's religious identity. In short, interchurch marriages comprise the ranks of "mixed marriages" who survive to become something more—families in which the divided churches have discovered a mutual interest.

The possibility of describing themselves as interchurch families has emerged with a steady momentum from the ecumenical breakthroughs of the past twenty-five years, particularly the dynamics set in motion by the Second Vatican Council's (1962–65) reforming principles for the restoration of unity between the churches. It is against that horizon that interchurch families grow in importance, as well as in numbers. To what extent can their claim of "double belonging" be appreciated in the context of the overall ecumenical picture? Why is conversion of one partner no longer the immediate solution urged by the church? How can churches respond to new questions such as the joint celebration of the baptism of children in interchurch families? What are the imperatives and needs for ecumenically sensitive religious education which interchurch family children personify? Is it possible that the sacraments of confirmation and first eucharist could be experienced as unitive, rather than divisive in an interchurch family? Can we identify patterns of pastoral care for interchurch families that reverse the malpractice which has caused interchurch couples to feel as if there is something wrong with their marriage? How have developments between the churches in dialogue created new possibilities even for eucharistic sharing? And, finally, have we begun to perceive interchurch families as a gift for the churches, as families whose experiences of faith and commitment to justice, human dignity, and peacemaking provide the converging churches with a concrete and lively example of a new paradigm for the restoration of Christian unity?

When the Glenmary Home Missionary Joe O'Donnell arrived in 1965 at his rural Morgantown, Kentucky parish, a new ecumenical fervor in Catholic culture prompted him to seize an initiative. He wanted to join the local Pastors' Evangelical Conference. After making the necessary contacts and attending their meetings, Joe voiced his desire to become a member of their ministerial association. "Brothers, there is someone here," spoke one of the pastors, "and we must face the issue, whether to admit a Catholic. We need to vote!"

It turned out that Joe lost the vote, 5 to 4. But he refused to be discouraged. Surely, he thought, in the next year I can change one vote. He determined to cultivate a friendship with the Baptist pastor. The man's wife voiced aggravation that he had voted against the Catholic priest. Joe invited them for supper, and over the course of a year the couple quickly became his close friends. At the end of the year the Baptist pastor intimated to Joe that he had learned a lot about Catholics and grown to appreciate his friendship. "Joe," he whispered, "this year I'm going to change my vote on your membership. This year I'm going to *abstain*!"

Anecdotes like this one expose how painfully hesitant we can be when it comes to ecumenical progress. But such humor, a healthy instinct for parables in the ecumenical movement, likewise gauges our liberation from behaviors that now seem like paralysis. Our ecumenical history has too often been one of abstaining when it comes to affirming a common baptism. And perhaps nowhere does the hesitation, the procrastination become more visible than in the lives of interchurch families.

This chapter will address the increasingly frequent phenomenon of interchurch families. It is all too easy to overlook the grassroots emergence of religious intermarriage in our culture. Official dialogues, formal meetings of church leaders, even ecumenical conferences can neglect the lived experience of married partners claiming different denominational identities. Our theological consensus statements offer new conceptual models for church unity. And yet they rarely reach the hands or ears of the assembled Christian communities they intend to serve. I prefer to describe interchurch families as ecumenism "with a human face" because their *experiences* manifest in less formal ways some of these same principles and possibilities of church unity. First we will look at some of the demographics, or statistical data, on religious intermarriage in the United States. Then we will review some of the pioneering work of two European centers in England and France.

Demographics

Sociologists and Family Ministry researchers continue to remind us that the gap between the "ideal" family and the "reality" of family life has metamorphosed dramatically in the past two generations. W.C. Roof and William McKinney rehearse the familiar statistics: one-fifth of all American families are now single-parent families; two-fifths of all American families have dual wage-earners, i.e. working mothers *and* fathers; one-tenth of all children in our society live in non-family arrangements.[1] The implications of these and other phenomena such as blended families of second marriages, single-child families, zero population growth, increasing numbers of out-of-wedlock births for women in their twenties and thirties, and child care are yet to be fully analyzed. Our pastoral theology has yet to integrate adequately the interchurch family identity into our "family systems" approach.

John A. Coleman has focused on the *religious* changes in Catholicism with startling revelations about family life. One in every five persons born Roman Catholic no longer affiliates with this church. Among Protestants, twice this number (two in every five) no longer affiliate with their original Protestant church—indicating remarkable fluidity in Protestant church membership.[2] The reasons for these changes in church identity vary. For some it is a matter of indifference and gradual dissolving of church contacts. Others identify questions of authority, experiences of community, pastoral care, or even stances of the various churches on political issues (pro *and* con) as the source of their religious migration.

Coleman, however, affords two additional perspectives. They are paradoxical. Eighty-five percent of Roman Catholics raised in a Roman Catholic family remain active in that church. But young Roman Catholics (age 18–29) are two-and-a-half times as likely as their parents (over age 50) to have married a non-Catholic. Put another way, 36% of Roman Catholics, age 18–29, have married non-Catholics; only 14.4% of their parents, age 50 and over, have married non-Catholics.[3] This has raised the issue of numerous "new family" denominational questions. How are these young religious intermarriages faring? Do both spouses declare a truce and mutually agree not to attend church because it might divide their marriage? Do they survive to become "interchurch marriages," with each spouse actively practicing in his or her church? Or does one spouse convert? Does each spouse take an active role in the religious education of children? What church identity, if any, do they decide for their children? On what basis?

Parallel statistics from intermarriage demographics are found in Dean Hoge and Kathleen Ferry's earlier (1981) research, where they report a 40% national rate of religious intermarriage.[4] Hoge refines this data in a more recent study where he analyzes a complex of "factors" operative in the new flexibility for Roman Catholics to marry non-Catholics. Four of the major factors are: (1) the dissolving of ethnic cultures which successfully had discouraged Catholics from marrying non-Catholics; (2) upwardly mobile Roman Catholics erasing the socio-economic factors that had effectively erected barriers to marrying non-Catholics;[5] (3) the increase in numbers of second marriages which are more likely to be with non-Catholics; and (4) the correlation of higher education and more mature age at marriage with the incidence of marriage to non-Catholics. Hoge poses the question: To what extent do "religious factors" impact a marriage more than these other factors which increase intermarriage? He concludes that *other factors,* such as education, no premarital pregnancy, no former marriage by the spouses, "taken together ... have much more impact on marriage survival than religious factors."[6] This conclusion reverses the bias that has discouraged Roman Catholics from marrying non-Catholics because that factor alone would threaten their marriage.

The University of Notre Dame's *Study of Catholic Parish Life (1981–88)* corroborates the statistics of Coleman, Ferry and Hoge. In comparing Roman Catholics in their twenties with Roman Catholics in their fifties, this study reports an increasing frequency of marriage to non-Catholics at a rate twice as high: 28% to 14%. An important characteristic of the Notre Dame research, however, is that its data are based on Roman Catholics who are actively involved in contemporary parish life. This would omit many of these couples and families who have been either alienated or marginalized from parish life. John Coleman's research hints that the incorporation of "baby boomers," who are disproportionately more likely candidates for interchurch marriage status, harbors a mixed message. The "homecoming effect" of these young adults who "return to the church as they marry and begin to raise families" mingles with a weaker commitment, as compared with their parents' generation. Coleman identifies "the precipitous decline in Catholic mass attendance": from a high of 74% in 1958, to 53% in 1985.[7] One suspects the rate for younger families as a subgroup is even lower than the general population.

One response to this data has been to jump to the conclusion that the blame for such lax participation belongs with "mixed marriages." It is easy to make a scapegoat of these families. As a matter of fact, however, truly *interchurch* couples and children often participate fully in both churches, even in leadership roles. Questions inevitably follow from a more objective observation. Is the incidence of religious intermarriage merely a matter of a new *laissez faire* ecclesial attitude, the free market traffic of marriage in a pluralistic culture? Could it be that Catholic-Catholic marriages are just as liable (if not more so) to excuse themselves from weekly mass? religious education of children? Or is it possible that young adults in interchurch marriages are making a quiet but profound ecumenical statement about their identity as members of the *one* church with distinct traditions, even though they continue to experience the scandal of divided churches? Could these interchurch families have navigated a paradigm shift that makes possible an experience of the future church in ways that old patterns of belonging and models do not afford the rest of us?

The American Context

Before we compare this United States phenomenon with interchurch marriage experiences in England and France, it will be helpful to acknowledge the uniqueness of American ecclesial life. We are a nation born in the wake of an extraordinary history of denominationalism. The spectrum of churches that has thrived in North America is unparalleled. On the other hand, the history of new schisms, new denominations born out of conflict within churches, and all too frequent proselytism (with all the negative connotations) in American religious history makes visible the shameful scars that have betrayed the ecumenical impulse for one body of Christ. Paul A. Crow, Jr. has recounted the paradox of the post-reformation missions in the new world. On the one hand, America offered relief from established churches and persecution; but on the other hand, our missions have transplanted our European churches' divisions. The voluntary principle, competition among denominations, and the flight from reason to pietism with its "heart" religion approach—all these contributed to "poor prospects of early Christian unity efforts," Crow surmises. His metaphor proves apt when he captures our new ecumenical attitude, not hostile toward each other, but like couples who have divorced and decided they could be still friends but nothing more.[8]

The sheer breadth of the spectrum of churches in America has compounded the ecumenical project for us. It is fair to say that we are at least a generation behind our European peers whose national experiences reflect predominantly *bilateral* configurations. For example, in England the established Church of England and the Roman Catholic Church have been able to address one another in dialogue and ecumenical cooperation as relative peers. In Germany, the established Lutheran Church and the Roman Catholic Church enjoy a similar parity. The established Reformed Church in France addresses the Roman Catholic Church as a cultural equal. These countries enjoy the luxury of a natural bilateral dialogue.

In the United States, however, the multitude of churches and their various judicatory or diocesan structures assaults one with a maze of institutional networks and bureaucracies. More to the point, our Catholic tendency to identify all non-Catholics as generic "Protestants" only contributes to the inertia of the ecumenical status quo. Ecumenism "with a human face," however, stands before us in the Methodist-Catholic, Lutheran-Presbyterian, Disciples-Baptist, or Catholic-Episcopal couple that is marrying. They personify a distinct, visible unity among our divided churches. The very lack of a dominant *pattern* in the identity of these potential interchurch couples has caused the churches to procrastinate about bilateral efforts to address and respond to the gifts and needs of these couples. It is for that reason that we can turn to the pioneering work of interchurch family ministry in two countries, England and France, where the preponderance of interchurch families has empowered these couples and their children to explore new possibilities and to progress toward new paradigms of church unity.

The British Experience: Association of Interchurch Families

Background

England enjoys a well-deserved preeminence in ministry to interchurch couples. In April 1968 six pioneer couples met in Sheffield at the instigation of a couple whose marriage was strained over the problem of how to proceed with the baptism of their first baby. This inaugural meeting was soon followed by an autumn weekend conference at the Dominicans' Spode House in Staffordshire where other couples and clergy were invited (a total of thirty persons). Thus the Association of Interchurch Families (AIF) was born.

The success of their enterprise is indexed by the growth of an extraordinary network. In 1970 thirteen regional English sites were initiated. Each has an official secretary who convenes local groups and reports on developments and maintains communication with the parent organization. "Sister associations" began in Ireland in 1973, and in Scotland in 1984; an Australian branch dates from 1968. AIF maintains a close association with the Northern Ireland Mixed Marriage Association (NIMMA). In 1980 the first international AIF conference met in Rydal, England. Subsequent biannual gatherings have been held in Corrymeela, Northern Ireland (1982 and 1990), Dunblane, Scotland

(1984), Dublin, Ireland (1986), and Lingfield, England (1988).

In 1979 AIF inaugurated a publication, the AIF newsletter, *Interchurch Families,* replacing the London group's mimeographed circular letter. The newsletter offers a semi-annual record of news, reports, feature articles, correspondence, and significant "Centrepiece" articles that address at length particular pastoral questions. The guiding forces behind AIF's genesis have been the visionary ministries of Martin Reardon (an Anglican priest) and his Roman Catholic wife, Ruth, and John Coventry, S.J. From its inception, interchurch couples who are Anglican or Protestant ministers and their Catholic spouses have proved unique catalysts. A circle of Jesuit ecumenists, following Coventry's leadership, have stimulated the Roman Catholic participation. Martin Reardon and Coventry co-chair AIF along with Ruth Matthews, a Baptist minister. In 1976 the association graduated to a higher profile when the Cardinal Archbishop of Westminster, the Archbishop of Canterbury, the Moderator of the Free Church Federal Council, and the Archbishop of Wales agreed to become its presidents.

Unique Identity: "Interchurch" Couples and Families

When AIF couples struggled to give a name to their movement, they made a unique contribution. Their founders' attention to a unique identity avoided the dense acronyms that ecumenical bureaucrats prefer. The term "interchurch marriage" was coined at the first Spode conference in 1968. The couples at this inaugural meeting resisted "mixed marriages" because it was not adequate to describe their experience. Such language applied as well to interracial and interfaith marriages. More importantly, the founding couples sought to distinguish their marriages from the "mixed marriages" in which only one or neither partner practices the faith.

In their 1980 Centrepiece article "What IS AIF For?" they began: "The Association of Interchurch Families is a focus for all concerned with marriages between committed Christians of different church allegiances (usually a Roman Catholic and a Christian of another Communion)—couples and families themselves, but also clergy, relatives, godparents, and all involved with their pastoral welfare."[9] Emphasis is placed on the family's commitment to unity in Christ, holding within themselves a loyalty to two, as yet separated, churches. Another Centrepiece article, "Mixed Marriages and Interchurch Families," reflected on this identity and ministry with an even greater maturity. Sixty-five percent of all marriages in England and Wales, they noted, involve a Roman Catholic and a partner who is not Catholic. The Roman Catholic bishops have estimated that no more than ten percent of these might be called "interchurch" marriages because one or both partners have been alienated from their church. This fact eventuated in a twofold emphasis: (1) "the specific mandate of AIF is for two-church families—where one Christian family has living relationships with two different churches . . . to involve ourselves as a couple in the life of both our churches, so far as we can, and to pray and work constantly for all that promotes unity between them"; and (2) helping mixed marriages (where one or both partners are non-practicing in the church) develop into an interchurch marriage, and avoiding the lapse of an interchurch marriage into a merely mixed marriage.[10]

Over twenty years of ecumenical history unfolds in AIF's self-reflections. Their primary emphases have grown with a consciousness that, while the churches are at present divided, most of them are seen on a continuum of convergence and commitment to the search for full visible unity with one another. The attitude of AIF couples, both of whom are practicing and committed Christians who belong to different churches, is one neither of "competition" (mutual unilateral decisions) nor of "co-existence" (couples simply agree to differ), but of "cooperation" (joint decisions, especially regarding religious education and ecclesial life of children) and "commitment" to unity. To use the language of AIF, these families experience themselves as a "domestic church" (*Lumen Gentium,* 11). Though sacramentally united in marriage, "their family unit is attached to two different churches, at present divided (although now recognizing themselves to be on a converging path towards unity)."[11] The couples live the ambivalence of their unity *and* tension, a reality acknowledged by Pope John Paul II at York, England in May 1982 when he singled out their unique role: "You live in your marriage the hopes and difficulties of the path to Christian Unity."[12]

In 1985 AIF again proclaimed the unique identity that had given birth to their association: the urgency of nurturing their children in faith. As on other occasions, AIF admitted that ten year intervals do not measure much time in ecumenical history. But "only a decade or two" spans their personal opportunity (and difficulty) to nurture children within the climate of an interchurch family.

> But many would testify to a joyful experience of duality and unity, outweighing all the problems and hurts. Thus they are raising not only questions of eucharistic hospitality, but underlying questions of double belonging, or "reciprocal ecclesial hospitality," of dual membership, especially for the children of such families. They are putting questions to the churches, and are ready to be questioned in their turn.[13]

In Chapters 3 and 5 we will pick up again the story of AIF and the neuralgic questions of sharing eucharist and the other sacraments of Initiation for interchurch families' children. It will become even more obvious that AIF has proved itself an articulate, intelligent advocate, reminding the churches by their presence and voice that they have committed themselves to restore full, visible unity. AIF excels in posing *the* ecclesiological questions occasioned by both interchurch marriage and the chain of ecclesial events that involve interchurch families: baptism, first communion, confirmation. AIF challenges and invites the churches to ponder the intrinsic ecumenical gravity of the very process of Christian initiation.

The French Experience: *Les Foyers Mixtes*

Background

Lyons enjoys a premiere ecumenical reputation among French cities. One immediately thinks of Abbé Paul Couturier whose theological pioneering and tenacity reached from Lyons to present the Week of Prayer for Christian Unity (an important evolution beyond the "Chair of Unity Octave") to the ecumenical movement. This style of "spiritual ecumenism" with its Eastern Orthodox overtones has flourished in what French ecumenists style "*la pastorale.*" The death of Couturier in 1953 coincided with the founding of the Centre St. Irénée in Lyons. His disciples' commitment to carry a vision for "unity in the manner that Christ wills" could find no better legacy than the activity and resources of the center named for Lyons' second century theological ancestor.

In October 1968 (simultaneous with, but independent of, the founding AIF conference) the ecumenical leaders at

Centre St. Irénée began publishing a quarterly bulletin, *Foyers Mixtes,* written and edited by interchurch couples with the collaboration of theological advisers. The editorial stance of the periodical combined both ecumenical information and reflection for a readership today of over two thousand subscribers. In the space of an average issue's thirty-four pages a variety of features appear: testimonies by interchurch couples; documentation of official statements or pastoral directives affecting the couples; letters and occasional responses; ecumenical models for sacramental celebrations and worship with couples. In 1973 the review, circulating mainly in France and French-speaking Switzerland, began publishing a list of regional correspondents to promote the publication and to coordinate ecumenical organization and activity centered around couples in each region. Over thirty such regions are now identified in France; eight throughout Switzerland; and corresponding couples in eight foreign countries: Germany, England, Belgium, Canada, Spain, Ireland, Italy, and Holland.

Thematic issues make *Foyers Mixtes* particularly useful. A glimpse at their scope fails to do justice, but indicates the style of the Centre St. Irénée's ministry to interchurch families: Catholicity; Eucharist: Bread Shared?; The Communion of Saints; Our Children: Awakening Faith; Mary: Living Faith; Paul: Free in the Spirit; John's Gospel: The Transfigured Christian; John the Baptist: Expectation; Becoming a Christian; Ecumenism: The Fruits of Dialogue; Catechesis; Privation and Sharing: St. Francis of Assisi and Peter Waldo; Double Belonging; Re-Reading *Baptism, Eucharist and Ministry;* Divorced . . . Remarried.

René Beaupère, O.P. is the visionary architect and director of *Foyers Mixtes.* Editorial responsibility rests with him, six interchurch couples and, since 1977, a Protestant theological adviser (currently, Heinz Blaser). *Foyers Mixtes* initially subtitled itself "an ecumenical bulletin of information and reflection." The primary readership has remained engaged and married interchurch couples, as well as priests and pastors who minister to them. The early subtitle was replaced by a new description in 1973: "information and reflections for a living ecumenism." The evolving identity of the periodical is evident in this 1973 self-evaluation: "It seems to us that this formula better describes our goal which is not to publish scholarly, abstract and timeless reflections, but more to avoid that the acquired ecumenical knowledge whose fulness stretches out each year remain frozen, to work at what happens in the concreteness of the daily life of our couples and thus of our churches."[14] This living experience of ecumenism in the reflections and testimonies of interchurch couples centers the content of *Foyers Mixtes*.

At times the editors have admitted that this methodology proves delicate. In a 1981 issue entitled "Daily Ecumenism" they acknowledged a recurring editorial stance: "None of the testimonies one will read is 'normative,' none constitutes a model," they cautioned. "It is a question of attempts more or less successful—and for which *Foyers Mixtes* does not intend to be totally accountable—providing different levels and diverse places of the Church's life." These are recorded, *Foyers Mixtes* said, "to give flesh to ecclesiastical documents and to stimulate widely the reflection and discovery—also the constructive criticism—of engaged and married mixed couples as well as priests and pastors."[15]

Double Belonging

Foyers Mixtes' advocacy role is nonetheless clear. In their 1981 fiftieth issue, the editors addressed the style of renewal proper to their review. "From inside the churches we wish to continue to challenge our responsible leaders, our communities, our brothers and sisters with our limited but significant experience: in our homes do we not live, at least partially, an anticipation of the one Church of tomorrow?" In turn, they noted, they accept the reciprocal act of being challenged.[16]

In an issue on the theme of "Structures of the Church," *Foyers Mixtes* considered the obstacles interchurch couples face vis-à-vis the institutional church. They rejected the common response of indifference, "letting the poor church collapse," and chose another solution: "to try patiently to be better acquainted with it, to love it, in order to play a role, with all the means of our strength, of animators, stimulators."[17] Here a comparison of *Foyers Mixtes* and the British Association of Interchurch Families reveals a subtle difference. Both groups acknowledge the minority status of interchurch couples who conscientiously continue to participate in respective churches and seek to raise children with an interchurch appreciation, participating in both parents' ecclesial lives. The *"foyers mixtes"* terminology differs from AIF emphasis on the "interchurch" identity of these marriages. The focus on the "home" ("foyer" translates literally "hearth" in French) and the "domestic church" is at least more explicit. There is no reluctance to employ the "mixed" reference.

What evolves in *Foyers Mixtes* reflections on the unique identity of interchurch couples is a twofold conviction: (1) couples and their families claim a "double belonging" (*double appartenance*); and (2) couples and their families do not create a "mythical third church." The first conviction raises ecclesiological questions and promotes a constructive theological and pastoral response. The second conviction, by contrast, seeks to rebut a recurring charge made against the implications and future directions of families who attempt to realize a "double belonging."

The theological acumen of René Beaupère equipped

Foyers Mixtes to explore the question of "double belonging" with a deft pastoral hand. His reflections are developed in the pages of *Foyers Mixtes* and in a lengthy 1980 article contributed as part of a festschrift volume for ecumenist Heinrich Stirnimann. American interchurch couples can profit immensely from Beaupère's thoughts on "this principal theme in ecumenism today."[18]

The term "double belonging" had achieved such acceptance in Swiss circles that the Roman Catholic bishops' diocesan commission for ecumenism (Lausanne, Geneva, Fribourg) published a November 1980 working text entitled "The Problem of 'Confessional Double Belonging.'" They made some general affirmations about the positive role of interchurch couples and their families (e.g. double registration as a concrete sign of mutual recognition of baptism). But the thrust of the official reply to the use of "double belonging" discounted it as "inadequate." In spite of couples' not wishing to create a "third church," the document said, they risk unconsciously creating such a church for the child by envisaging such a "double belonging" by mandating an ecumenically integrated catechesis. The commission charged that this redirects the churches to a "common denominator," rendering the urgency of working for the rapprochement of the churches less comprehensible.

While Beaupère applauded the commission for four affirmations, he distanced himself from their text on two points. First, he criticized their notion of the church as too static and institutional. Second, he asked if the problematic of the commission is not "all or nothing"? Would it not be a more nuanced understanding, he asked, to consider "degrees" of belonging? "Imperfect communion" between churches could be more positively understood, he reminded. Stages or steps *toward* full communion would then follow. Beaupère admitted that the expression "double belonging" is not perfect. He uses it for lack of a better one. He does not, he emphasized, wish to say by it what we speak of in the sense of a "double agent." It does not mean to belong to *neither* church. Nor does it imply that the engagement with one community is of the same order or intensity, nor that one is admitted and sharing all that is said or lived in each of the two. His cogent conclusion deserves a lengthy quotation:

> But the expression "double belonging" witnesses to the truth that our churches are linked in depth by the Spirit of Christ and by his gospel and that the full unity to come will not be forged politically by a learned and balanced assembly of the different structures of the Christian communities, but rather spiritually, by an interior osmosis which will allow my brother—also bearer of the Spirit—to live in me, and the evangelical values witnessed to by his community to penetrate my own ecclesial cell.
>
> It would not be wrong to transpose the famous tag of Terence: *christianus sum, christiani nihil a me alienum puto.* Because the spouses and children of a mixed marriage are Christians, nothing of what is Christian is foreign to them. They *can* participate in all the evangelical values which are manifest in the two mother churches. Moreover, they *ought*—with others and more than others—to be the conjunctive tissue which closes the edges of the open wound of the *one and only church* of Christ. For this they belong to two churches which are still "denominationally" distinct but in the process of becoming—with them, through them, and in them—the *one church* of tomorrow.[19]

A later response by Beaupère to the ongoing discussion appeared in the issue of *Foyers Mixtes* entitled "Double Belonging." He had already begun to suggest that he would "more gladly" employ the expression "reciprocal ecclesial hospitality"[20] as a more exact expression. He appealed to the precedent of "provisional anomalies" which had historical precedents in the life of the church. And in his 1980 essay, Beaupère explained that "reciprocal ecclesial hospitality" intends "not to say less than 'double belonging,' but to pass from the juridical-canonical plane to the biblical." The dramatic shift away from the terminology to a new expression bears careful scrutiny.

> When I say hospitality, I see the fact that I am at home, truly at home, in many of the places of the church and at the home of members of the church which are not mine. But I see, above all, the hospitality living in the Jewish people and in scripture. I think of Abraham receiving the three angels. It is marvelous that in French the term "host" designates at the same time the one who receives and the one who is received. Abraham receives God under the form of the three angels but at the same time God receives Abraham. There is reciprocal hospitality between them.
>
> I love also that hospitality makes the appeal, almost of itself, to sharing the meal. This is the narrow line which exists between ecclesial hospitality and eucharistic hospitality. The two realities are named one after the other.
>
> Whereas "belonging" has connotations more banal, more superficial and, in another way, more juridical. I do not much love to say that I "belong" to the church. I have a membership card to a party or a society. The church is in me and I am in it. It is of another order.[21]

Just as in the Association of Interchurch Families, in *Foyers Mixtes* circles the foundational questions opened by the identity of interchurch families have led to new questions about the nature and future of the church. In Chapters

3, 4, and 5 we will pick up the story of *Foyers Mixtes,* exploring how issues like "double belonging" and "reciprocal ecclesial hospitality" have intensified and taken on new meaning in the context of the neuralgic question of sharing eucharist and *Foyers Mixtes* children celebrating the sacraments of Christian Initiation. In many senses, *Foyers Mixtes* has responsibly articulated a "copernican revolution"[22] in our understanding of ecumenism and the pastoral possibilities for restoring the unity of the church.

Concluding Observations

This chapter began with an overview of the phenomenon of increasingly frequent intermarriage between Christians from different denominations. The statistics reveal a seismic shift in a cultural pattern which had effectively maintained strict religious boundaries for centuries. The xenophobia that segregated believers into denominational tribes appears now to have virtually reversed itself.

Questions cluster around this development. How many of these religious intermarriages survive to become truly "interchurch"? What proportion of these marriages and families are alienated from both partners' churches? Why? What efforts at evangelization and welcoming do the churches venture? What can we learn from the pioneering efforts of English and French interchurch groups?

Observers of the ecumenical movement repeatedly have attempted to measure the pace and rhythms of church unity. Albert Outler offered in 1986 the much-quoted remark that bureaucratic ecumenism was "dead still" in the water.[23] A decade earlier Charles Moeller of the Vatican Secretariat for Promoting Christian Unity reported on a gap between *official* ecumenism, which was "congealed" and at a "standstill," and *grassroots* ecumenism which seemed to be "running wild."[24] The failure to integrate these two dimensions of ecumenism has plagued the churches. And yet, if the ecumenical movement is, as Pope John Paul II said within days of his election as bishop of Rome (and has repeated at regular intervals), "irreversible,"[25] the official church's ecumenical policy and the grassroots inevitably must converge for the sake of authentic Christian unity.

We began this chapter lamenting the everyday hesitations that in effect once stalled the ecumenical breakthrough. We must turn in the next chapter to the lived experience of crisis points and hurdles which potential interchurch couples must anticipate and negotiate in order to emerge with their unique gifts for the church's pilgrimage to unity.

Notes

[1] W.C. Roof and William McKinney, *American Mainline Religion: Its Changing Shape and Future* (New Brunswick: Rutgers University Press, 1987) 155–57.

[2] John A. Coleman, S.J., in Thomas M. Gannon, S.J. (ed.), *World Catholicism in Transition* (New York: Macmillan, 1988) 237.

[3] Ibid. 243.

[4] Dean R. Hoge and Kathleen M. Ferry, *Empirical Research on Interfaith Marriage in America* (Washington, DC: USCC, 1981).

[5] David Leege, director of the University of Notre Dame study of Catholic parish life, has observed that in the U.S. "the GI bill (providing free college tuition for veterans after World War II) may have had more of an impact on the Catholic church than the Second Vatican Council" (Coleman, 235).

[6] Dean Hoge, *Converts, Dropouts, Returnees: A Study of Religious Change Among Catholics* (Washington, DC: USCC/New York: Pilgrim Press, 1981) 73–75, 76–77, 80.

[7] Coleman, 241.

[8]Paul A. Crow, Jr., *Christian Unity: Matrix for Mission* (New York: Friendship Press, 1982). Cf. Martin Marty, *Righteous Empire: The Protestant Experience in America* (New York: Dial Press, 1970); R. McBrien on "factionalism" as an expression of this same dilemma, *Caesar's Coin: Religion and Politics in America* (New York: Macmillan, 1987); and Michael Kinnamon, *Truth and Community: Its Limits in the Ecumenical Movement* (Grand Rapids: Eerdmans, 1988).

[9]*Interchurch Families* 3 (June 1980) C1-4.

[10]*Interchurch Families* 12 (Winter 1984–85) C1-4.

[11]*Interchurch Families* 3 (June 1980) C1.

[12]*Interchurch Families* 7 (June 1982) 1.

[13]*Interchurch Families* 12 (Winter 1984–85) C1.

[14]*Foyers Mixtes* 18 (January 1973) ii. (All *Foyers Mixtes* translations in this book are my own.)

[15]*Foyers Mixtes* 53 (Oct.–Dec. 1981) 4.

[16]*Foyers Mixtes* 50 (January–March 1981) 4.

[17]*Foyers Mixtes* 36 (July–September 1977) 3.

[18]*Foyers Mixtes* 52 (July–September 1981) 31. Cf. *Unterweig zur Einheit* (Wien: Editions Universitaire, 1980); an English translation appeared in *One in Christ* 18 (1982) 31-43.

[19]Ibid. 33.

[20]*Foyers Mixtes* 54 (January–March 1982) 40.

[21]*Foyers Mixtes* 59 (April–June 1983) 20-21.

[22]Karl Rahner, "The Active Role of the Person in the Sacramental Event," *Theological Investigations* 14 (New York: Seabury, 1976), 161-84.

[23]"Ecumenism 'dead in water': CMSM told," *The Chicago Catholic* (August 22, 1986) 3.

[24]As quoted by René Girault, "The Reception of Vatican II," *The Reception of Vatican II,* ed. Giuseppe Alberigo (Washington, DC: The Catholic University of America Press, 1987) 149.

[25]John Paul II, "The Inaugural Homily," *Origins* 8 (November 2, 1978) 3.

2. Crisis Points and Hurdles— Interchurch Marriage Preparation

When an interchurch couple moved to their new neighborhood, the Episcopal wife and Roman Catholic husband began the search for new churches where they would gather for worship. Once they found pastors who seemed ecumenically sensitive, the question of a pattern for Sunday liturgy surfaced. Because the mother found an excellent religious education program for children at the Episcopal church (and the Roman Catholic parish offered nothing outside of mass), she usually took her nine and six year old daughters there on Sundays. The father customarily went to the Roman Catholic church, and joined them for a brunch outing afterward. Several months had passed when the pastor of the Episcopal church greeted the mother in the vestibule and remarked to her that the congregation had a group for single parents and the widowed. He invited her to join them. "My husband's not dead!" she exclaimed. "He's just a Roman Catholic."

The lived experience of engaged couples poses a multitude of sometimes awkward practical crises and hurdles when the couple wishes to claim an interchurch identity. Pastoral questions and patterns of care are set in motion with their initial contact with their churches, to prepare for the wedding liturgy. The initial "problems" associated with all marriage "preparation" must be examined in the context of possibilities of surviving as interchurch married partners. And yet there are few, if any, absolute solutions for inter-church couples. The vignette just narrated illustrates how interchurch families can begin and remain often virtually hidden, marginal, even anonymous in a community of faith.

The demographics of our first chapter hint that the churches have yet to discover or address a vast new arena for pastoral care. This is not to say that they will need to invent a spectrum of new interchurch programs, but that they must make the whole gamut of pastoral and educational pro-grams in the churches more inviting and responsive to the identity of interchurch families, as well as for the majority of families they already serve. The greatest mistake would be further marginalizing them, or denying the whole church the opportunities to benefit from interchurch families' faith and gifts.

By titling this chapter "Crisis Points and Hurdles" I deliberately intend to question whether the churches' vari-ous ministers, ordained and non-ordained, respond to inter-church families with authentic "care" (grounded in *caritas*), the genuine *love* that marks the community of Jesus. One extreme is illustrated by the experience of a newly married interchurch couple who recounted their search for two churches, each of which would be open to the Roman Cath-olic and Evangelical partner. They had found such a parish for the husband. And they thought that they had finally found a corresponding church for the wife. Upon introduc-ing themselves to the pastor after the morning's worship, however, the minister reached a welcoming arm around the husband and announced, "We have lots of ex-Catholics here!" At the other extreme is the wedding liturgy in which the pastor decided to resolve the issue of sharing eucharist for a Roman Catholic groom and independent Christian church bride by offering communion only to the couple. Thinking that he was sparing the visible division of the congregation, he had trivialized the fullest expression of eucharist as the participation of the gathered body, the church. Why not a wedding liturgy without eucharist? Far better to maintain the integrity of the church's sacraments than to contradict their intrinsic meaning.

By the same token, ordained and non-ordained professional ministers are not the only ones expected to offer pastoral care and avoid malpractice with interchurch families. As we will explore, interchurch wives and husbands must make serious decisions about the religious identity of their children. The attitude of procrastinating, or letting each child decide his or her church tradition at some adolescent or teenage moment, equally constitutes malpractice on the part of interchurch parents. Psychologists and religious educators agree that the formative, early pre-school years of life are critical for children's healthy religious development. Opinions, even among ecumenists, vary as to what extent children can be nurtured in *both* parents' traditions. But to neglect any responsibility as the primary religious educators, however difficult a particular decision might be for parents, approaches a form of child abuse.

Martin Reardon has captured the residual effects of pastoral malpractice in a memorable story. In England a young boy had prepared to serve his first mass at the Roman Catholic parish. It was to be an early, weekday morning liturgy. So his Anglican father drove him to the church and was greeted by the small community gathered in the front pews. At communion time the proud father impulsively felt the need to receive. He followed the others to the priest, where his son was holding the paten. The priest refused to give the man communion. As every Roman Catholic priest knows, this refusal contradicted every pastoral directive, as well as prudent judgment by the priest. We do not refuse people in this circumstance who present themselves for communion. One might seek them out for a conversation afterward, but a priest does not refuse or embarrass such a person on the spot. To this day, years later, the son has never returned to church because of the rejection and humiliation his father suffered.[1]

This chapter will examine pre-marriage preparation for interchurch couples by analyzing four distinct and potentially divisive topics: (1) the question of the conversion of one of the spouses; (2) dispensations for a Roman Catholic to marry another Christian; (3) the nature of "the promises" made by the Roman Catholic spouse; and (4) the wedding preparation and liturgy for an interchurch couple.

Initial Questions for Interchurch Marriage Preparation

The Christian faith of engaged partners offers the foundation for sacramental marriage. But few couples on the threshold of marriage have the opportunity to reflect directly and systematically upon the content or form of their faith. The staffs of Family Ministry offices around the country and the overwhelming majority of priests, deacons, and pastoral ministers report reservations about the preparedness of many people—even partners from the same tradition—who seek to marry in the church. It is only fair to remark the coining of a new term "baptized unbelievers" to describe this dilemma.[2] While people may have been baptized in the church, and even may have celebrated first eucharist and been confirmed, they regularly lack the catechesis and mature faith development the church expects. In some cases more and more young people have not had the ethos of a parochial grade school or religiously-sponsored high school education. Others have neglected participation in the church during college and early career years when they are mobile, repeatedly transplanted, and lacking in the ongoing experience of a parish or faith community.

This problem is not peculiar to interchurch couples, though they are often scapegoated as the culprits responsible for what is wrong with marriage these days. To compound the problem, many couples seek marriage in the churches with which they have little or no immediate experience, or they borrow the family identification with their parents' church for the wedding. Various efforts to cultivate a minimal faith commitment such as a six month or one year waiting period before marriage in the church are rooted in these factors.

In the case of engaged interchurch couples, the unexamined understandings of different faith-backgrounds must ultimately be explored or the relationship will fail to mature religiously. Marriage depends upon a constellation of factors: personality-types, values, career choices, children, external variables such as health, and the mature freedom to nurture an authentic commitment. An extraordinary honesty and acceptance by partners proves essential throughout the relationship. Couples face grave matters of conscience that affect their married life. Some of the issues which interchurch couples find helpful for engaged couples to discuss are:

—What "expectations" do you bring to your marriage as an interchurch couple?
—What "apprehensions" do you bring to your marriage as an interchurch couple?
—Do you anticipate any particular positive or negative experiences surrounding marriage preparation or the ceremony?

—Describe the family attitudes toward your interchurch marriage: at the time of your engagement; in your planning for the wedding; as you imagine your marriage at five year intervals.

Engaged interchurch couples have a decided advantage over engaged partners coming from the same church tradition. They cannot presume anything about their intended spouse's religion or religious practice. They naturally inquire about, compare, and contrast the importance of religion, religious differences, and beliefs held in common. Some of the questions interchurch couples find helpful for engaged interchurch couples to discuss are:

—How devoted are you to your local parish or congregation?
—Do you feel a definite responsibility toward it, or is your attachment to it a matter of social convention with little deeper significance?
—What do you think about your church's stand on the great moral and political issues of the day? about my church's stand?
—Do you have doubts about the faith that the church teaches?
—Do you think that by marrying someone of a different tradition and outlook you will be betraying what your church stands for?
—To what extent does the church influence your daily life?
—Is your faith an inclusive, joyful experience that can transcend denominational boundaries or a formal observation of rules and conventional behavior?
—What do you think about my religious beliefs?
—How much significance do you attach to the ecumenical movement?

—What doctrinal differences of the churches impinge upon our relationship?

—How will our decisions about family planning integrate each of our churches' doctrinal positions and our own exercise of conscience?

As one interchurch couple warned, engaged couples need to become aware of "the importance of incidentals" in one another's religious practice. Does grace offered before meals mean a great deal or little to you? Is Christmas midnight mass unthinkable or indispensable? Despite differences, both experiential and doctrinal, the couple should always emphasize the foundational truths they hold in common, especially their faith in the redemptive life, death, and resurrection of Jesus Christ. It is in the intimacy of their prayer and life together that they will deepen that common faith and be strengthened for a lasting marriage.

Conversion

Previous generations found a common solution to interchurch marriages by promoting the conversion of either husband or wife (in fact, more often the conversion of the husband whose faith was culturally considered weaker and less evident than the wife's, or the conversion to the stricter church discipline, e.g. to Roman Catholicism). It was routine pastoral practice to recommend that "for the sake of the marriage" it would be preferable for a conversion to occur. These arrangements of convenience continue to be promoted in some pastoral circles.

It is helpful at this juncture to return to our definition of an interchurch family. Recall that such husbands and wives actively participate in their respective churches. They are each conscientious and committed to their distinctive tradition of Christian faith, and to their parish or congregation. It would be empty or less than honest for these truly interchurch partners to transfer membership to their spouse's church for the superficial reason of convenience or appearances' sake.

Let me dramatize the repercussions of such an artificial conversion. Shortly after *The Louisville Times* published a page one story on a 1983 research report which I co-authored, revealing that nearly one-half of Roman Catholics in the Archdiocese of Louisville were marrying non-Catholics, I received an unsolicited letter. The woman who wrote the letter was obviously in a happy interchurch marriage of some duration. She orients us to the key to any successful marriage, particularly an interchurch marriage:

> A few months ago I read an article in *The Louisville Times* about the report you wrote concerning "ecumenical marriages." The article went on to say that according to the report few major problems were found in ecumenical marriages. But of course. Each partner in such a marriage begins on equal footing, with his pride intact. With all due respect, the report you should write is one on the marriages in which one partner gave up his/her religion at marriage to become what the other one is. This is what generates resentment, hurt pride and any number of bad feelings over the years.
>
> For a marriage to be based on the premise that one partner is "wrong" and has to be changed to be made all right to marry the other one, is no good at all as I see it in retrospect. It is very damaging to one's self-respect over the years. I feel sure young people are not encouraged to go into marriage in this way nowadays; but a study of people who DID a few years back might bring forth a lot of interesting responses, and relieve a lot of people of duodenal ulcers.

A veteran interchurch couple once cautioned to a pilot group of families, reflecting on their unique experience: nominal conversions with the intention of "saving" the marriage are only laying the groundwork for *misery* later. This brings us to two critical insights. First, truly interchurch couples recognize one another as responsible, believing Christians. They acknowledge one another as persons with different faith traditions which complement more than contradict each other. Because they are baptized into the one Christ, there is no necessity for either of them to "convert" to Christianity. And, second, it is inappropriate and inaccurate to speak of the "conversion" of most spouses in either "mixed" or interchurch marriages. One converts to God and to Christ, not to a particular church or tradition. This insight is corroborated when Roman Catholic parishes *refuse* to include baptized spouses in mixed marriages within the catechumenate process (otherwise identified as RCIA). The Roman Catholic Church speaks of receiving into "full communion" persons baptized in another tradition. Ecumenists continue to insist on this distinction. It reflects the understanding of the church articulated by the Second Vatican Council, a carefully nuanced teaching which we will reflect upon at length in Chapter 7. The abuses in parishes, which habitually (for pragmatic reasons) group unbelievers with believers from other Christian traditions in a common catechesis, prove to be at least ecumenically unethical, and doctrinally heretical.

In instances where a sincere desire by a husband or wife in an interchurch marriage for "full communion" genuinely occurs, pastoral ministers must respect the conscience of such decisions. Nonetheless, in facilitating a person's discerning whether or not such a commitment to the tradition of a spouse is authentic, it is not unreasonable to raise the threshold for those who are contemplating "crossing over."

They should be made aware of the possibility of doing the right thing for the wrong reason. They should even be challenged to discern whether their attraction to the spouse's church responds to a deep interior faith motive, or whether they are accommodating for the sake of convenience. It is even prudent to challenge whether they might mask an indifference to religious faith, an indifference disguised in the attitude that one tradition is equivalent to another.

Interchurch families prefer to envision the ongoing conversion of each member of the family, growing in the understanding of Christ's call to a fuller, more mature faith life. Not least in that responsible discipleship is a realization of their contribution to the ministry of ecumenism, working for visible signs of the church's unity. But it also involves for them the conversion of the institutional structures of the church, even envisioning the church's role in the social, political, and economic restructuring of the world according to the principle of the dignity of the human person. Interchurch couples converge with Christians from diverse traditions to witness their continual *conversion* through servant ministries and reconciliation.

Dispensations

The history of the sacrament of marriage fascinates theologians because it evolved to its current form only in modern time. Many of the symbols of marriage come from the pre-Christian, imperial Roman betrothal and marriage ritual: rings, kiss, bridal veil, and exchange of vows, as well as the crowns which are still used in Eastern Orthodox churches. What has remained central is the principle that the marriage is made by the exchange of consent by the husband and wife themselves. The couple ministers the sacrament, one to another. This alone constitutes a valid marriage. Therefore the couple are not "married by" an ordained minister, but they marry themselves. With Christianity's fourth century ascendancy as the imperial religion, the church began to exercise legal responsibilities in regard to marriage. By the medieval period, abuses had crept in through some Christians entering clandestine marriages and later denying that they had exchanged consent without witnesses. As Alasdair Heron chronicles this Romeo and Juliet syndrome, such a loophole was opened until the Council of Trent's "remarkably ingenious solution." On November 11, 1563 the council's decree *Tametsi* obligated Roman Catholics from that point in time to exchange consent in the presence of the priest and two or three witnesses for a valid marriage. "The presence of the priest and witness does not of itself make or add anything to the actual marriage; rather, it is a *precondition* without which the exchange of consent cannot take place."[3] This became known as the "canonical form," the manner in which marriage, according to the laws (or canons) of the Roman Catholic Church, would be expected to take place. The intent was to place marriage in a social and faith context of the gathered community of faith. The effect, however, in Heron's words, was to cast the Roman Catholic Church's pastoral concern in legal form, to emphasize control rather than care.

A subtle implication of the sixteenth century decree *Tametsi* was the failure of the Roman Catholic Church to recognize Protestant marriages as valid, sacramental unions. What was to be said for those Protestants who "converted" (in the language of the times) to Roman Catholicism after their marriage? The historical plot thickened because of European idiosyncrasies. For example, the Netherlands implemented the conciliar decree under Spanish rule as a Roman Catholic country. But when the Netherlands became independent and Protestant, interchurch marriages became common. To complicate matters, Protestants appealed to have former marriages annulled on the grounds that they had not observed proper canonical form, i.e. marriage before a priest and witnesses. In 1741 Pope Benedict XIV issued the declaration, *Matrimonia quae in locis,* otherwise known as the *Benedictina.* He ruled that Protestant and interchurch marriages in the Netherlands were valid even if the canonical form had not been observed. Thus, *Tametsi* applied only to marriages between Roman Catholics.

Heron summarizes the "untidy situation" which culminated in the 1908 decree *Ne Temere* and the 1918 Roman Catholic *Code of Canon Law.* Because there were locations where *Tametsi* had not come into force and was not binding, or because of modifications such as the 1741 *Benedictina* arrangement, the happenstance of geography, in effect, determined the issue of "canonical form" as a requirement for valid marriage.

> [*Ne Temere* (1908)] brought in a single set of regulations for the whole world except Germany and Hungary. . . . [T]hey made the canonical form a condition of validity for all marriages involving a Roman Catholic, but not for any other marriage. . . . The position was thus less tightly controlled than under *Tametsi,* but more tightly than under the *Benedictina;* for while all non-Roman Catholic marriages were exempt from the form, mixed and interchurch marriages involving a Roman Catholic were bound by it. This is why *Ne Temere* is often thought to have been chiefly concerned to impose restrictions on interchurch marriage; but in fact it did so only indirectly. Its real aim was to standardise the regulations for all Roman Catholic marriages. But of course, in areas where *Tametsi* had either never come into force, or subsequently been relaxed by the provisions of the *Benedictina, Ne Temere* imposed fresh and stricter rules on in-

terchurch marriages than those which had previously operated. Hence its reputation even to the present day, particularly in Ireland, where in parts of the country at least the situation before 1908 had been much less strictly controlled.[4]

Only with this background can the dispensations ("permissions") be understood. There are two categories of "impediments" (obstacles) to mixed or interchurch marriage in current Roman Catholic Canon Law: (1) a "disparity of cult" impediment which arises when the non-Roman Catholic party is not a baptized Christian (cc. 1086, 1129); and (2) a "mixed religion" impediment which arises when the non-Roman Catholic party is a baptized Christian of another tradition (cc. 1124–28).

The historic roots of these dispensations are found in the abuses of medieval clandestine marriages, and in conciliar and papal documents discussed earlier. The rationale behind the dispensations is to guarantee the conscientious faith commitment of the Roman Catholic spouse to his or her church. It does not imply a negative or judgmental decision about the non-Catholic spouse, in keeping with the Second Vatican Council's positive statements about non-Christians and other Christians living outside full communion with the Roman Catholic Church.[5] It intends to motivate the Catholic to participate and grow in the Roman Catholic tradition. Such dispensations can be arranged by the pastor (or associate, deacon, or other pastoral minister) and have become a routine process.

The dispensation for a marriage liturgy outside a Roman Catholic church is technically called a dispensation from canonical form. The church laws (canons) oblige a Roman Catholic to exchange his or her vows before the authorized Roman Catholic ordained minister (bishop, priest, deacon) or lay minister (if authorized)—ordinarily the parish pastor or associate—in a Roman Catholic church. "If serious difficulties pose an obstacle to the observance of canonical form" a dispensation may be requested (c. 1127). In the United States, the most frequent appeal to dispense from this requirement comes from the cultural custom of the marriage liturgy taking place at the church building of the bride. Thus, the minister at that church would preside at the exchange of vows. Other reasons might warrant such a dispensation, e.g. a couple marrying at the college/university chapel where they attend could have reasonable grounds to request that location and the campus minister to preside. Like the previous dispensation, this is routinely arranged.

Before leaving this question, a characteristic Roman Catholic practice should be noted. Every person seeking marriage in the church is required to secure a copy of his or her baptismal certificate, ordinarily issued within the last six months. A similar proof of baptism is needed from the non-Catholic Christian. This process relates to the definition of marriage as a sacrament expressed through the vowed commitment by two baptized persons. It also serves to defend the bond of marriage by recording in the baptismal records any sacramental marriages a person covenants.

But this does not prohibit malpractice on the part of some pastoral ministers. One possible problem concerns the difficulty in securing baptismal certificates from some other churches. Many have less elaborate record-keeping than Roman Catholic parishes. Others are unfamiliar with such certificates and might be asked instead for a letter certifying the baptism's date and place. When dealing with other churches, it might be more effective to ask the minister of the non-Catholic Christian to request the certificate or letter from his or her denominational colleague if the baptism took place out of town. It is a temptation for a Roman Catholic priest or pastoral minister to seek a dispensation from the impediment of disparity of cult when a proof of baptism proves elusive or less than convenient. But the implications of that stroke of the pen are staggering. It (canonically) deprives the marriage of its deeper sacramental reality. It denies the recognition of the other spouse's baptism. At the very point when the church should celebrate the potent, visible recognition of a common baptism, such a dispensation vitiates this foundation of the marriage sacrament. Here lurks a subtle, menacing form of malpractice.

"The Promises"

When the oral history of the modern ecumenical movement is recorded, a special volume needs to be reserved for the saga of nineteenth and twentieth century interchurch couples who weathered dehumanizing, often offensive, and indifferent pastoral practices associated with the Roman Catholic Church's "promises" required of spouses in a "mixed marriage." The Roman Catholic Church officially discouraged such unions. (Other churches had equally negative attitudes toward "mixed marriages," though they rarely formalized them in such official documents.) This polemic reached its apex in 1830 when Pope Pius VIII's letter, *Litteris altero,* simply declared as an absolute that "outside the true Catholic faith no one can be saved," thus obligating Roman Catholics in "mixed marriages," by divine law, to ensure to the extent humanly possible that children were formally initiated into the Roman Catholic Church.

Failing to dissuade a couple from marriage, the church required that both the Roman Catholic party and the spouse from the other church sign a promise that all children of the marriage would be baptized and raised as Roman Catholics. The church grudgingly resorted to perfunctory parlor weddings, denying the marriage party the celebration of the sacrament in the church's worship space. The indignities remembered and narrated by faith-filled wives and husbands from other churches are invariably juxtaposed with an appreciation of the change in official Roman Catholic Church attitudes.

The historical scars that both the churches and individuals bear from this unilateral Roman Catholic claim are manifold. Since Pope Paul VI's 1970 apostolic letter *Matrimonia Mixta,*[6] this abrasive agent has dissolved. In most countries, and particularly in United States dioceses, the other Christian is advised of the Roman Catholic promise, and it is not necessary for the other Christian to promise or sign any document. While some national conferences of Roman Catholic bishops continue to require a signed commitment for the Roman Catholic party, an oral promise (and not a signed promise) is common.[7]

Alasdair Heron frames his analysis of the promises on the broader claim that requirements of canonical form have on *every* Roman Catholic's ecclesial life. This is a point easily lost in assessing the promises. Indeed, pastoral practice might be termed disproportionately lax when examining, in fact, how the obligations to baptize and raise children of Roman Catholic–Roman Catholic couples in the faith and liturgy of their own church apply. In a publication of the Irish Association of Interchurch Families, Heron writes with clarity on the deeper, unresolved sources of the promises:

> The basic cause of the interchurch marriage situation does not lie in the fact that members of one church may marry members of another. It lies in the fact that the churches are divided from each other in the first place. Were there no such divisions, then interchurch marriage

would not exist.... It is interchurch division which is the root cause of interchurch marriage.

This means that it is superficial and unjust for people to talk, as they sometimes do, as if it were the fault of the interchurch couple themselves that they have these problems to face. They are in fact victims of a situation they did not themselves create. The thing which is really wrong, the fundamental anomaly, is not that a Roman Catholic and a Protestant should get married, but that the churches should be so separated from each other that marriages across the divide run into these difficulties.[8]

In the deliberations of the Second Vatican Council (1962–65), *The Decree on Ecumenism* introduced new understandings of the ecclesial identity of other baptized Christians, as discussed under "dispensations" earlier in this chapter. A second document of the council, the Declaration on Religious Liberty, a distinctively United States contribution by John Courtney Murray, called for a political guarantee of religious freedom as preferable to historical concordats and appeals for church privileges in diverse states. But the irony, unforeseen by some, was that this very freedom of religious conscience could not be claimed without extending it to others. One of the most important beneficiaries of this document would be interchurch families. Now, the Roman Catholic promises, if unilaterally forced, could compromise the responsibility and freedom of the other Christian spouse in the marriage. Indeed, that spouse has an equivalent freedom and responsibility to participate and contribute just as conscientiously as the Roman Catholic to the children's religious education and faith formation. The decisions involved ultimately will be part of the marriage dynamic and process. The promise in no way could foreclose on the evolving new possibilities as the couple and the churches progress, en route to the implementation of the restoration of "full communion."

It cannot be denied that in some instances the anti-ecumenical, unilateral malpractices surrounding the promises continue to linger in too many pastoral circles. Couples are abusively given only half the story. But a more sensitive pastoral attitude has gradually become commonplace. This threshold of marriage preparation can become a potent point of entry for interchurch couples who seek to be responsible about remaining faithful to their respective churches, but who rightly claim the religious freedom guaranteed by the Roman Catholic Church. In the context of their sacramental marriage they exercise a holy discernment and decision-making.

Because the 1985 interfaith marriage guidelines of the Archdiocese of Cleveland are a clear and succinct model regarding the true intent of the promises, they merit an excerpt:

1. Only the Catholic person is asked to promise anything; the person of the other religious tradition is simply asked to be aware of the promise made by the Catholic.
2. The promise is not absolute. It should be understood as it is stated. Does it mean that the Catholic spouse will determine how the children will be raised with no recognition of the wishes or conscience of the other religious tradition? Certainly not. A helpful way to consider the promise is to see it as a commitment of the Catholic party that if for any reason the upbringing of the children were left entirely up to them alone, they would see to it that the children be raised and educated as Catholics.

3. It is not sufficient to simply promise that the children will be baptized and raised as Christians. This is to be a specific commitment on the part of the Catholic party. The importance of the promise is that the Catholic person make a specific commitment to continue practicing the Catholic faith. Further, that this personal commitment to the faith is strong enough that it is seen as an important value worth being passed on to the children. If the Catholic person is unwilling or unable to make such specific commitments, then it would be consistent to recommend that the Church recognition of the proposed marriage be delayed until such time that the Catholic is able to commit themselves (sic) as described above.

4. Catholics should be aware that the above promise is to be understood in the light of the developing relationship of the Catholic Church to other Christian churches begun by the Second Vatican Council (1964) and continuing today under Pope John Paul II. . . .[9]

Leonard Pivonka has termed the transition, from a limited religious tolerance prior to the Second Vatican Council to contemporary ecumenical initiatives, an "overturn[ing] in principle." And yet he concludes that the attempts, from *Mixta Matrimonia* through the 1983 *Code of Canon Law,* to harmonize the discipline concerning interchurch marriage with the council's sensitive, ecumenical understanding of the church were not fully accepted in church legislation.[10] The Anglican/Roman Catholic International Commission's 1976 report on interchurch marriage addresses this issue with two important emphases. First, the appeal of the church to "divine law" applies the Roman Catholic's obligation to his or her own faith, and not to the ecclesiastical discipline of the promise. Second, the Catholic party is

required to provide (*pro viribus*) for the Roman Catholic
education of the children in the marriage as far as possible
(*quantum fieri potest*), a duty "circumscribed by other duties
such as that of preserving the unity of the family." Mutual
rights and obligations in the specific marriage situation
must be weighed, respecting "the equal rights in conscience
of the non-Roman Catholic party" lest the marriage itself
be endangered.[11]

Wedding Preparation and Liturgy

Parents and the Extended Family. The immediate reaction of some parents, sisters and brothers, grandparents,
godparents, and the wider family of aunts, uncles, and
cousins (and even "significant other" friends) matters immensely to an engaged interchurch couple who announce
their marriage. The ideal response is a complete, uncon-
ditional love for the couple. But even when this happens,
afterthoughts can temper the initial joy of a son or daughter's announcement if the ecumenical conversion has not
yet touched a person. In some instances an immediate negative response can dishearten the couple. Even though the
climate of denominational segregation and bigotry has
waned over these past twenty-five years, earlier generations
carry suspicions, doubts, mistrust, and outright hostility
about the restoration of the unity of the churches. Nothing
can so discourage the engaged interchurch couple as the
hesitation or disappointment voiced or detected during
those initial days of their decision to marry.

The first step for the engaged interchurch couple is to
anticipate this potential problem. Their respect and concern
for parents and others can be demonstrated through a willingness to invite them into a discussion about the issues and
how they themselves have addressed them. The couple does

not abdicate their own responsibility and initiative. They provide a teachable moment, a climate for understanding. They become catalysts for others' attitudinal change. If the interchurch identity is envisioned as a positive factor by the couple, they can allay fears or worry. No parent or anyone close to the bride or groom wants anything to harm them. Initial alarm should not be misread.

Priest, deacons, and other pastoral ministers prove an enormous support for parents and others at such a moment. Their friendship with the family affords a unique pastoral presence that reinforces positive ecumenical values at the personal level. Without denying the difficult decisions and pioneering witness exacted from the couple, the pastor (and others) can disabuse parents of the notion that their son or daughter's marriage is any lesser in the eyes of the church. Grace is the experience of their married love: God is present, transforming the couple in the love, and in their life with one another. In fact, the pastor (and others) might raise the consciousness of the family to the role interchurch couples play in the church's progress toward full communion with the other churches.

Issues of paramount concern to parents are the baptism of grandchildren and their religious education. They need to be heard and reassured of the couple's fidelity to their own church and the new possibilities opened by interchurch families. Because these issues are felt strongly on both sides of the family, the social meeting of in-laws early after the engagement (if it has not already taken place) affords an opportunity to reassure everyone of the conscientious commitment of the couple. They need to get to know one another. An agenda of religious issues for discussion may or may not be appropriate, but should always be secondary to the sensitivities of everyone. There is nothing guaranteed to stir as much anxiety for a couple on their wedding day and thereafter as rival expectations projected between in-laws. Interchurch marriage preparation attends to this dynamic in a way that can be envied by other families.

Consulting the Clergy/Planning the Wedding Liturgy. With candor and humor, an ecumenical couple described their marriage preparation with the minister and priest involved in their wedding as "our joint pastoral care for the clergy!" Myths and negative attitudes about ecumenism and interchurch marriage continue to linger in some pastoral circles—irrespective of age or geographical locale. Couples report coming from rectory discussions with the pastor, under the impression that "something was wrong with us." However, this residue of resentment and implied judgments of failure directed at engaged interchurch couples has, by and large, dissolved.

Three factors affect the quality of help engaged interchurch couples are likely to receive:

(1) How ecumenically-minded and ecumenically-active are the clergy?

(2) How familiar are they with changing church regulations and pastoral possibilities for interchurch couples?

(3) How pastorally sensitive and sympathetic are they to the difficulties and gifts of truly interchurch couples and families?

Guidelines for different pairings of interchurch couples repeatedly advise at least one joint pastoral session with clergy or others, to review and discuss the churches' expectations and pastoral possibilities for them. This ideal rarely happens. Its omission is symptomatic of an overworked clergy and other pastoral care-givers. This fact should not minimize the possible orientation such an investment of time and preparation can give an interchurch couple for their married and family life. The invitation for both clergy to participate in the wedding liturgy powerfully symbolizes this reality, and should not be overlooked where warranted by the commitment of truly interchurch partners. I would venture to say that in the lives of most who attend interchurch wedding liturgies, this can be their most potent and positive collection of ecumenical experiences, indeed the source of a new consciousness.

Many Roman Catholic dioceses have relied on marriage preparation programs to relieve individual priests from some of the pastoral burdens, especially in parishes where numerous marriages are celebrated. These series of evenings, or day-long workshops, parish-based married couple-to-engaged couple preparation, or weekend Engaged Encounters serve the majority of engaged Roman Catholics and their partners. It will be more and more important that these structures be ecumenically responsive in the future, as we cultivate the attitude that interchurch marriages are a gift to the churches, just as holy and worthy as the marriage between two Roman Catholics. Segments of these programs will need to address interchurch questions and possibilities. Already a few have integrated elements of this dimension. But the work of interchurch couples as leaders and peer-couples involved in this ministry promises a new moment for pastoral ministry and ecumenism.

There are numerous protocol issues that affect two churches and the priests or ministers who nurture an interchurch marriage. Since the 1970 document *Mixta Matrimonia,* the participation of the other church's minister (or the Roman Catholic priest, deacon, or pastoral minister's participation) in the wedding liturgy, the gathering of the community to celebrate in the Roman Catholic worship space, and the blessing of the marriage by the priest all contribute to a more positive attitude. The only principle that is axiomatic is for the priest/minister whose church is the location of the ceremony to preside and receive the vows. When eucharistic sharing is not possible (the neuralgic question to be explored next, in Chapter 3), it is necessary to celebrate a non-eucharistic wedding liturgy in order to symbolize the unity of the couple, and not burden this celebration with the division of the churches made obvious by only one of the spouses (and usually only half of the community) receiving communion.

Summary

This chapter has tackled the difficult crises and hurdles which potential interchurch couples confront in preparing for their marriage. Sensitive pastoral thresholds will respect the desire of truly interchurch partners to maintain their identity within their respective church traditions. We have explained why the kneejerk recommendation of past decades, that one spouse automatically convert to the church of the other, no longer can be honestly promoted. The developments in Roman Catholic requirements for dispensations to marry another Christian were analyzed in the wake of the 1970 ecumenical change of direction which created new possibilities for celebrating the sacramental covenant, grounded in a common baptism. The complex historical Roman Catholic "promises" made by the Catholic partner in any mixed marriage were carefully interpreted and demythologized as they apply to interchurch marriage and the religious liberty of both wife and husband. Finally, the pastoral care of the extended family of an engaged interchurch couple led us to recommend a broader meaning for pre-marriage preparation as a teachable ecumenical moment, and the occasion for a fuller participation in the wedding liturgy by both families and both circles of friends. But as our next chapter reveals, the couple has only just begun.

Notes

[1]Martin Reardon to Louisville, Kentucky chapter of American Association of Interchurch Families, December 5, 1989, Cathedral of the Assumption.

[2]See Susan Woods, "The Marriage of Baptized Nonbelievers," *Theological Studies* 48 (1987) 279–302.

[3]Alasdair Heron, *Two Churches—One Love* (Dublin: APCK, 1977) 31 (italics mine). I rely on Heron's study for many important details in the historical development of interchurch marriage, particularly medieval and post-Trent church law. For more recent developments see Leonard Pivonka, "Ecumenical or Mixed Marriages in the New Code of Canon Law," *The Jurist* 43 (1983) 114, where he emphasizes that "canonical form was a practical response to the long history of clandestine marriages" pre-dating the historic divisions of the church, and should not be misunderstood as a counter-reformation discipline directed against non-Catholics.

[4]Ibid. 33–34. See esp. chapter 2, "Marriage and the Churches," pp. 23–37 and chapter 3, "Roman Catholic Treatment of Interchurch Marriage in the Past—the Codex Iuris Canonici," pp. 38–45.

[5]Commentators on *Nostra Aetate*, the Declaration on Non-Christians, and *Unitatis Redintegratio*, the Decree on Christian Unity, emphasize how those documents obligate Roman Catholics to this new attitude. George Tavard comments that the double expression "church and/or ecclesial communities" used in the decree is consistent with *Lumen Gentium*, n. 15, which emphasized "the solidarity of all Christians" and does not mean a negative judgment on what could be a church and what could only be an ecclesial community. It was inspired by the close ties seen by Catholic theology between ecclesial communion (or church) and eucharistic communion. Where one recognizes the eucharist, one recognizes a church. This was the working principle adopted by the council. But the council did not wish to pass judgement on where Catholics recognize or do not recognize the Eucharist. ("Reassessing the Reformation," *One in Christ* 19 [1983] 361.)

[6]*Acta Apostolicae Sedis* 62 (1970) 257–59.

[7]Cf. J. Makothakat, "The Directories of Episcopal Conferences Implementing Matrimonia Mixta," *Studia Canonica* 13 (1979) 303–38 for a revealing comparison of diverse Roman Catholic episcopal conference directives. This diversity, chronicling both rigorist and more ecumenically progressive policies, is itself a classic study of modern Roman Catholic diversity on the international scale. It quickly exposes the true catholicity of the episcopal conferences and local churches (dioceses).

[8]Heron, 14.

[9]*Guidelines for Interfaith Marriages* (Cleveland: Archdiocese of Cleveland, 1985).

[10]Pivonka, 118.

[11]*Information Service* 32 (1976) 23 (articles 58–59).

3. Pastoral Care of Interchurch Families

An interchurch father defended his children's double belonging under pressure from a newspaper reporter during an interview for a feature story in the diocesan paper. When the journalist kept returning to the newsworthy suspicion that some church officials might be less than pleased with children (or adults!) who claim a double belonging, the father grimaced. He refused to answer definitely when asked to *which* of the two churches his older daughter belonged. "That's a question for the churches. You tell us!" he challenged. "And we really want to put the monkey on the churches' back. It should be on their back, not ours!" he declared. How the churches respond to this fact of interchurch families' experience of double belonging ineluctably determines the depth and quality of their ongoing pastoral care.

As we surveyed in the last chapter, the churches have traditionally focused attention on marriage preparation and the wedding liturgy of an interchurch couple, but neglected pastoral after-care of the family. The survival of interchurch couples depends on both their own initiative and the pastoral ingenuity of parishes and congregations. Needless to say, to reverse the hemorrhaging of so many potential interchurch families away from the church will depend on a delicate balance of both factors. And responsive pastoral care can motivate a couple to begin the process of committing themselves to respective churches, keeping them from the all too common alternative of abdicating any church identity or responsibilities. Churches and pastoral ministers need to develop clear and certain invitations to interchurch couples. They have an obligation to nurture them so couples are not attracted to the apparent solution of letting their interchurch marriage deteriorate into an a-religious union. This chapter will address (1) patterns of interchurch family participation in the churches, (2) double belonging, and (3) possibilities for eucharistic sharing by interchurch families.

Patterns of Participation

Interchurch couples face unique decisions about their church identity. Their marriage preparation concentrates on immediate practical questions: from who is going to manage finances, to writing thank-you's for wedding gifts, to finding and decorating a place to live. Even if they anticipate ecumenical questions affecting their life, these pale into items for procrastination. One couple in a pilot group of interchurch couples recounted their confusion and anxiety on the first Sunday after the honeymoon trip and moving to their new home. "Where would we go to church that first Sunday?" the wife asked herself. To her dismay, both she and her husband had "presumed that you would accompany me to church." Because they had not discussed or anticipated such an inevitable question, she said, we had set ourselves up for that very tension we wanted to imagine as impossible in our ideal marriage.

At the beginning of their married life, *all* couples bear an acute sensitivity to their unity. They scrupulously avoid anything that threatens to divide them. It may mean spending less time with in-laws, or cutting ties with old circles of friends or interests. That instinct can be natural and healthy. But the question that confronts interchurch couples only magnifies as they begin their relationship: Now what does the wife/husband *expect* of each other's ongoing church identity? A husband from another pilot group offered an analogy from his own professional work as a high school alumni director. The churches, he suggested, have to maintain contact with interchurch married couples. "It's a matter of 'keeping them involved' and not losing touch," he surmised.

The phenomenon of newly married couples immediately being transplanted to new neighborhoods or new towns and cities is a virtually universal factor. They lose contact with their home churches and rarely continue to be part of the local parish where their marriage liturgy was celebrated. In many cases, the couple had only a marginal connection with that parish to begin, through a family connection. The engaged couple may have been away for four years of college, military service, or launching a new career. It is not uncommon for adults during those years to be less conscientious about church identity and participation. Some have even lapsed into the category of baptized unbelievers. In short, the marriage celebration can occasion the couple's reentry to the practice of faith. But even for the activist interchurch couple, the threshold for crossing into a new community of faith presents a difficult step. Not only are they invited to seek a "home" parish for each of them, they are faced with discovering a pattern for their church identity as a couple.

Each interchurch couple makes decisions about the husband's and wife's parish or congregation. They decide to what extent they will be involved with one another's church.

They anticipate how any children will fit into their church identity. These are complex decisions. They grow out of the ongoing process of their marriage relationship. One couple candidly appraised their situation and asked, "Are we gluttons for punishment?" "We're starting with a built-in gap," said the husband. "We're consciously working harder to stay closer—and that means you can't get lazy about your interchurch identity." His wife added, "You don't have to agree, you don't even have to compromise, *you have to talk!*"

Each interchurch couple, like every married couple, will develop a singular pattern of church participation. The accumulated experience of pioneer couples can orient others to a spectrum of models. Here are several patterns of church identity which veteran interchurch couples have considered and live.

Full participation in both churches. Many couples initially make heroic efforts always to accompany one another to church every Sunday. This "duplication," they usually find, becomes exhausting and in many ways unnecessary. For one, it seems to imply a judgment against the other's church. It can also offend liturgical sensibilities with a redundancy that makes one wonder how "present" one can be to oneself in such a Sunday morning marathon. However, for couples who find they are unable to partake of communion at their partner's church, and need this weekly, a double attendance fulfills their need. It is important to note that this pattern rarely survives (for obvious reasons) after the birth of children.

Alternating between churches. One of the most common patterns for interchurch couples finds them on alternate Sundays at one another's church. This allows the couple to participate at church every Sunday as a couple. (Few interchurch couples find it meaningful or satisfying to attend separate liturgies on Sunday, although some regularly attend a Saturday evening Roman Catholic eucharist, and then the Sunday morning liturgy at their partner's church.) This pattern maintains an ongoing presence in both churches, allowing them to be known and get acquainted with members of each community. Perhaps most importantly, these couples become identified at their churches as an interchurch couple with unique gifts and needs.

Finding a "magnet" church to serve interchurch needs. As couples mature in interchurch consciousness and articulate their needs, more and more appear attracted to a single parish or congregation which can minister to their interchurch identity. This does not mean that the other partner surrenders participation in his or her church. Nor does it preclude some form of occasional presence at the other church. But it does evidence that couples seek out and respond to ecumenically sensitive pastors, pastoral ministers, religious educators, and parishioners. Such "magnet" parishes or congregations satisfy social, educational, and spiritual needs. They are even more likely to promote a visible ecumenical life with the gifts of interchurch couples being appreciated and utilized prominently in that church's ministry. Interchurch families are known to commute great distances and make other sacrifices of time and treasure to participate in such a church.

Whatever pattern an interchurch couple eventually chooses, they are nearly unanimous in recognizing that their household dialogue and everyday sharing of prayer, devotional practices, religious traditions, and discussion of faith and/or church issues have equipped them to be more knowledgeable in one another's tradition, as well as in their own tradition. Many interchurch couples boast that their personal experience as an interchurch couple has challenged them to reflect upon and appropriate faith at more mature levels than couples from the same tradition who take so much for granted.

Double Belonging

A concept which has encouraged some interchurch couples is the description of their marriage as a "double belonging." The French ecumenist René Beaupère, O.P. has popularized and promoted this self-description by interchurch families. It enjoys a currency in European circles (France, Switzerland, Germany, England) where the *Foyers Mixtes* groups have an elaborate network with publications and conferences since 1968.

Beaupère grounds the concept for double belonging (*double appartenance*) in a theology of baptism. Baptism is the sacrament of initiation into the one Christ. It is by virtue of a mutually recognized baptism that the churches speak of a *sacrament* of marriage—a faith commitment to the unity of husband and wife which renews their baptismal covenant. So not only by virtue of a common baptism, but now compounded by the sacrament of marriage, interchurch couples claim a greater degree of belonging to one another's church. At the heart of this claim is the Second Vatican Council's understanding of the nature of ecumenism as the project of restoring the "full communion" between separated Christian churches. While Beaupère admits that this will be achieved in stages, he suggests that interchurch couples and their families have taken accelerated steps which warrant a double belonging,[1] a term we introduced in the first chapter.

While many are inclined to applaud Beaupère for his theologically cogent argument, the concept of double belonging is not without critics. European acceptance and appropriation of the understanding is widespread, and signs of its welcome in the United States are evident. However, two frequent criticisms are aimed at the concept: (1) "imperfect communion" between our churches does not permit a formal "double belonging"; and (2) interchurch couples risk unconsciously creating a "mythical third church" and abandoning their own churches. To the first criticism, Beaupère has replied that too static or institutional a concept of the church contradicts our Second Vatican Council teaching. He reminds that "imperfect communion" between churches can be *positively* understood—it is not a matter of simply "all or nothing," but a "real" communion between churches. To the second criticism, he suggests that practices such as double registration of the baptisms of children of interchurch families and their joint religious education and catechesis strengthen the churches. This does not, he insists, mean to belong to neither church. It may imply that the engagement with one community is *not* of the same order or intensity, and that one is not admitted and does not share all that is said or lived in each of the two. Nevertheless, there is a degree of "belonging" to both churches by virtue of the interchurch marriage.

This provocative suggestion, based on the Second Vatican Council's ecclesiology, undoubtedly will focus much future reflection about church identity of interchurch families in Europe, the United States and Canada. (We will return to double belonging in the reflections of Chapter 8.)

Possibilities for Eucharistic Sharing

The neuralgic question in ecumenical circles ever gravitates to the same issue: Could we somehow celebrate together the eucharist? All baptized Christians have a spiritual need for the eucharist. In word we are gathered to hear the proclamation of God's saving mercy, and at the table we give thanks and praise for the transforming power of the Holy Spirit and Christ present among us under the elements of consecrated bread and wine. This dynamic source and summit of Christian life continually nourishes and sustains us. Indeed, the eucharist is the sacrament of the unity of the church. We make visible our solidarity in faith and in the mission of the church as servant.

Whether in a parish church, or a diocesan, national, or international celebration, we experience the mystery of becoming the body of Christ when the eucharist is celebrated. Unity builds on a plethora of diversities. Who has not witnessed the power of the eucharist to heal the brokenness of factions, to overcome competitiveness, even to reconcile rivals in religious communities, parishes, or larger contexts? It is because we lack a perfect or ideal unity that we find that we repeatedly need the eucharist.

Pope John Paul II met at Warsaw with representatives of thirty-one Christian confessions of the Polish Ecumenical Council on June 8, 1987 and emphasized that only a church united in the eucharist will be a credible sign of unity and peace. His talk emphasized a common baptism and the realization that only the Holy Spirit can overcome existing divisions. The pope took the occasion to quote approvingly from the World Council of Churches' Faith and Order Commission 1982 report, *Baptism, Eucharist and Ministry,* a symbolic gesture all the more powerful, given the locale, in his native Poland. Among the quotations from *BEM* were two particularly significant ones from the eucharist section of the document: "We are constantly subject to judgement because of the persistence of multiple divisions and confessional conflicts within the Body of Christ" (n. 20); and "The fact that Christians cannot come together in full communion around the same table to eat the same bread and to drink from the same chalice weakens their missionary witness, on both the individual and community level" (n. 26).[2]

One of the most potent understandings of this dynamism of the eucharist found expression in the Second Vatican Council's Decree on Ecumenism. It is no coincidence that ecumenists have pondered how to implement its insight in light of the real, but imperfect, unity we share as baptized Christians and churches committed to the restoration of full communion.

> As for common worship, it may not be regarded as a means to be used indiscriminately for the restoration of the unity among Christians. Such worship depends chiefly on two principles: it should signify the unity of the church; it should provide a sharing in the means of grace. The fact that it should signify unity generally rules out common worship. Yet the gaining of a needed grace sometimes commends it.
>
> The practical course to be adopted, after due regard has been given to all circumstances of time, place, and personage, is left to the prudent decision of the local episcopal authority, unless the bishops' conference according to its own statutes, or the holy see, has determined otherwise (*UR*, 8).

The council captured the twofold dynamic of the eucharist: (1) it is a *sign* of the unity which already exists; and (2) it is the *means* to enable a new unity from our diversity, even to overcome our divisions. Such a dialectical understanding of the eucharist has enabled ecumenists to speak in terms of a "discriminate" celebration of the sacrament as an appropriate means to restore unity. This would not be the "general" practice of common worship, but the legitimate "gaining of needed grace" commended by the council.

Since 1967 the Roman Catholic Church has developed a series of official statements on possibilities for eucharistic sharing. Without attempting an exhaustive analysis of the documents, I intend to trace the development and its application to the life of interchurch families.

Terminology

The most important knowledge for interchurch families and those who minister to them concerns their ongoing worship life and a careful distinction of terms related to the eucharist. In this regard, a nuanced and informed appreciation of some of the subtle terminology can help avoid potential misstatements and improper requests. For example, it is inappropriate for an interchurch couple to request "intercommunion" because that would imply a formal, official agreement between two churches that indicated a resolution of all doctrinal issues which would otherwise impede a joint celebration of the eucharist. Some churches do have a policy of "open communion," or admission of any baptized person to receive communion. At the other extreme is "closed communion," or forbidding any person who is not a professed member of that local church or congregation to receive communion.

Roman Catholic teaching and practice, as reflected in the excerpt from the Decree on Ecumenism, can only be appreciated in the context of the commitment to restore "full communion" with all the churches. Ambitious as that goal might seem, it should never be compromised or eclipsed in presenting the church's authentic teaching. We have already alluded to theologians such as René Beaupère, who has reminded us that the "imperfect" unity we already share is a real unity which ought not to be denied in an "all or nothing" attitude. Such an understanding locates the Roman

Catholic Church's complex but progressive teaching on possibilities for limited eucharistic sharing. One often finds this concept of "eucharistic sharing" or "eucharistic hospitality" to indicate a particular occasion and specific circumstances in which a baptized person from another church might receive communion in the Roman Catholic Church. It holds an obvious application to the wife, husband, or child of an interchurch family.

Theological Reflection

Avery Dulles has appraised this same conciliar text vis-à-vis the lack of ecclesial unity among different confessions by suggesting: "Eucharistic sharing may at times be an appropriate sign of a growing, though still imperfect unity, and may under such circumstances confer a corresponding grace to move toward greater unity."[3] His sanguine reading of three post-conciliar documents, the Vatican's 1967 *Ecumenical Directory,* and the Secretariat for Promoting Christian Unity's 1972 "Instruction on Admitting Other Christians to Eucharistic Communion" and subsequent 1973 "Note" interpreting that instruction, concludes that the Roman Catholic Church then was moving "toward greater strictness." The mentality of these documents (and restrictions on local bishops) looked upon eucharistic sharing as undesirable, "an evil not to be permitted without serious justifying reasons."[4] Dulles questioned the necessity of the conditions laid down by the official statements, and suggested that "a certain liberalization" would have "the advantage of bringing the directives into closer alignment with what many conscientious and committed Christians are now doing, and would thus tend to make such persons better disposed toward church authority and toward ecclesiastical legislation."[5]

Three theological responses by Dulles to this early Vatican policy remain helpful. First, he acknowledged certain specific occasions (he mentions a "mixed marriage") when one might welcome other Christians to receive communion, even though "it would be anomalous regularly to receive communion in a church to which one did not wish to belong." Second, in assessing whether such persons have a faith in harmony with Roman Catholic teaching on the eucharist, "the demands should not be so stringent that believing Catholics would be excluded by the same tests." In Dulles' words, "A correct worshipful attitude is more important than an exact theological expression." Third, and finally, he cautioned about the difficulty of drawing up "specific rules applicable to all cases" in the religiously diverse United States. He suggested "directives, rather than laws" and considerable discretion in their application which "might appropriately be left to the local pastor or celebrant."[6]

Simultaneous events in Europe were precipitating some of the very Vatican reactions Dulles has analyzed.[7] The most celebrated instance was the November 30, 1972 directives for eucharistic hospitality for interchurch families, promulgated by Léon Arthur Elchinger, Roman Catholic bishop of Strasbourg, France. Because of the numerous interchurch marriages with French-speaking Lutherans and Reformed Christians in his diocese, Elchinger sought to respond to their spiritual needs for eucharistic sharing and to avert these *foyers mixtes'* alienation from the church. He carefully made two limiting statements as a context for his directives: (1) there can at present be no question of general intercommunion; and (2) one cannot presently authorize intercelebration/concelebration, or a jointly presided eucharist. Within the categories of "eucharistic hospitality" norms, Elchinger proceeded to issue a statement that Avery Dulles has said in his mind "admirably coincides with the teaching of Vatican II":

> [A Roman Catholic receiving communion in a Protestant church] would recall that certain deficiencies exist—greater or lesser according to the particular church—on the plane of the sacramental organism by which the Church visibly constitutes itself as the Body of Christ.
>
> He would know, however, that in spite of these deficiencies, those who celebrate the Eucharist in faith and fidelity to the Lord's testament may really share in the life of Christ who gives himself as food for his own for the building up of his one Body.[8]

This question of *reciprocity* in eucharistic sharing proved a lightning rod for Vatican reaction. Elchinger had already departed from the 1972 Secretariat for Promoting Christian Unity's Instruction on two accounts: (1) he extended the concept of "serious spiritual need" to include a need to foster the growth of ecumenical community; and (2) he omitted the requirement that a minister of one's own community should, in every case, be unavailable. Nonetheless, on March 1, 1975 the Swiss Interdiocesan Synodal Assembly adopted Elchinger's directives, and they were subsequently approved by the Swiss Roman Catholic Episcopal Conference.[9] In 1978 the French bishops' Commission for Unity issued positive directives for interchurch couples.[10] This was followed in 1983 by a document, "Eucharistic Hospitality with Christians of Churches Issued from the Reformation in France,"[11] which affirmed that (1) eucharistic hospitality cannot be habitual; and (2) eucharistic hospitality can be envisaged in certain exceptional cases. An effort was made, paralleling Elchinger's careful reflections, to emphasize the intrinsic relationship between church and eucharist.

It is important to note that in 1976 and again in 1981 the German bishops' synod issued a statement analogous to the 1975 Swiss text. It had addressed the reality of a Roman Catholic asking to receive communion from a minister who had not been validly ordained. Should such a Roman Catholic be convinced that conscience authorized her or him to do so, "this step should not be interpreted as necessarily implying a rupture with his own church, even though common sharing of the Eucharist remains problematical as long as the separation of the churches continues."[12]

The entire matrix of pastoral care for interchurch families rightly gravitates to this enervating question of eucharistic sharing.

Canonical Developments

In 1983 the Roman Catholic Church promulgated a revised *Code of Canon Law*.[13] This project had been one of Pope John XXIII's explicit goals, but took nearly twenty-five years to accomplish. It replaced the 1917 Code, and incorporates a wealth of theological renewal. Of central concern is the understanding of the church reflected in the new Code. John A. Alesandro has remarked, "The Revised Code can be a pastoral opportunity for us as a tool of ecclesial reform." His thesis bears scrutiny. Canon lawyers interpret the principles of church law and discipline, and advise members of the church on how those principles are applied in the life of the believing community. Alesandro, in concert with other canonists, has reminded us that Pope Paul VI charged the Code commission in 1965 to reform canon law, saying: "It must be accommodated to a new way of thinking proper to the Second Ecumenical Council of the Vatican, in which pastoral care and new needs of the people of God are met."[14]

The new ecumenical vision of the church embraced by the council has deeply colored the new Code's directives. One of the most subtle but relevant shifts concerns the new Code speaking more inclusively of the rights of "Christians" (for example, c. 205),[15] all those baptized, and not merely Roman Catholics. It reflects the profound recognition of a certain, but imperfect unity expressed in the Decree on Ecumenism and the Constitution on the Church. The application of the consequences of this ecclesiological shift to the pastoral care of interchurch families incubates in the new Code.

The canons on eucharistic sharing are a good case study of how the principles of church law are implemented. John Alesandro has captured some of the intricacies of interpreting the law with an illustration. In Italy he once observed a man standing underneath a sign which said: *vietato fumare* ("smoking prohibited"). Coming from an American culture, with its British common law tradition of absolutes, Alesandro reports that he informed the man that the sign meant he was not permitted to smoke his cigar. The man disagreed. He explained, from his point of view: "*Vietato fumare* does not mean that I cannot smoke or you cannot smoke. It means: what would happen if everyone smoked?" While Alesandro admits he may have overdrawn the contrast a bit, such a gulf between Roman law traditions and the British common law traditions exists.[16] One might find no better example than the complex Roman Catholic policy on eucharistic sharing.

James H. Provost has carefully assessed this question, with an emphasis on Anglican-Roman Catholic relations, in the 1985 Joint Standing Committee report of Episcopal and Roman Catholic ecumenical officers, *Food for the Journey.* He traces the post-conciliar documents (which we analyzed above), noting the broadening of what could be considered cases of "urgent need" for other Christians seeking the sacraments of eucharist, penance, and anointing of the sick. With the new Code of 1983, however, canon 844 provides a new context and source for addressing the question of eucharistic sharing. Paragraph 2 of canon 844 addresses Roman Catholics seeking the sacraments from non-Catholics:

> Whenever necessity requires or genuine spiritual advantage suggests, and provided that the danger of error or indifferentism is avoided, it is lawful for the faithful for whom it is physically or morally impossible to approach a Catholic minister, to receive the sacraments of penance, Eucharist, and anointing of the sick from non-Catholic ministers in whose churches these sacraments are valid.

The issue of validity or ordination narrows the possibilities, because the Roman Catholic Church recognizes only the validity of orders in the Orthodox churches. And because the Orthodox churches have declined the holy see's overtures for intercommunion until issues of authority are resolved, this section of the canon remains largely hypothetical.

In the case of other Christians seeking sacraments from Roman Catholics, paragraph 4 of canon 844 states:

> If the danger of death is present or other grave necessity, in the judgment of the diocesan bishop or the conference of bishops, Catholic ministers may licitly administer these sacraments to other Christians who do not have full communion with the Catholic Church, who cannot approach a minister of their own community and on their own ask for it, provided they manifest Catholic faith in these sacraments and are properly disposed.

While continuing what Provost terms "the cautious approach to sacramental sharing evident in conciliar and post-conciliar documents," he also finds some interesting developments. His outline of the *conditions* under which other Christians may receive these sacraments of the Roman Catholic Church deserves to be quoted with a detailed outline:

1) The person must be baptized. Baptism is necessary to be considered a Christian by the Catholic Church, and is the necessary prerequisite to receiving any of the other sacraments.

2) The situation must be one of serious need. This is judged in light of the traditional criteria of danger of death or "other grave necessity."

3) The judgment of what constitutes "other grave necessity" is proper to the diocesan bishop or to the conference of bishops. Either could make ad hoc determinations in individual cases, could delegate the determination to other persons, and can even make general norms to cover recurring types of cases. In making this determination, "grave necessity" is to be understood in the broader meaning given it by the Secretariat for Promoting Christian Unity in 1972. . . .

4) The other Christian must be in a situation in which access to a minister of their own community is not possible. This phrase is standard in the post-conciliar directives. It can be interpreted, however, in light of the context in which it appears in the code. Thus, the impossibility may be physical, or it could also be moral. . . . Of special note is the absence of the qualifier found in previous norms, that this access be impossible "*diu*"—i.e. for a "rather long" or "notable" period of time. It is not the chronological inability to have access, but the spiritual inability that is at stake here.

5) The disposition of the individual requesting the sacraments must be appropriate. That is, they must ask
on their own accord, not as a result of pressure from
others (including the Catholic minister); their faith
in the sacrament must be the same as that of Catholics; and they must be properly disposed.[17]

Provost makes several interesting notes on the underlying purpose of spiritual benefit to the other Christian seeking the sacrament. A helpful reminder is that "the faith
requirement [5, above] is in the sacrament as Catholics
believe in it, not necessarily in all the Catholic Church
teaches about everything."[18] From a canon lawyer's perspective, Provost includes a summary of the current Roman
Catholic position, recognizing that the principle of reciprocity continues to prompt dialogue in the development of
any new norms of eucharistic sharing. His sober conclusion
returns the question of eucharistic sharing to the pastoral
arena: "The task of pastors and ecumenists, however, is the
much more difficult one [than the canon lawyer's] of moving with the Spirit in our common quest for that unity for
which Christ prayed. Hopefully, the law will prove to be an
aid and not an obstacle in this process."[19]

In a more recent happening, Provost has called attention to the *Guidelines for Receiving Communion,* developed by
the National Conference of Catholic Bishops' Committee
on Pastoral Research and Practices and adopted on November 8, 1986 by the bishops' Administrative Committee. These
Guidelines have been widely published in missalettes and
hymnals in Roman Catholic parishes in the United States.
While Provost recognizes the "brief capsule" nature of the
document, he raises the question "whether the *Guidelines*
accurately reflect current church law on these matters," particularly in the second part directed "For Other Christians."

Twice in his commentary, Provost asks if the *Guidelines* are "too succinct." While the text limits itself to excluding a "general invitation" for other Christians to receive communion in the Roman Catholic Church, it does not afford the broader context of eucharistic sharing developments we have reviewed earlier.

Provost concludes that the current discipline of the Roman Catholic Church is "more complex than the statement in the United States bishops' *Guidelines* would make it appear." He emphasizes that it is not true that on a case-by-case basis other Christians are always excluded from the eucharist. In this regard, he reminds pastoral ministers: (1) that the guideline is pastoral advice, not a law or general norm; (2) the guideline does not replace the rightful responsibility of diocesan bishops in this matter; and (3) the new NCCB *Guidelines* fail to mention the present discipline of the Roman Catholic Church in regard to particular cases (canon 844). Provost sees a positive benefit from such an awareness in the opportunity for individual bishops issuing local directives "to clarify the application locally of the general church discipline in regard to eucharistic sharing." Or bishops might delegate such power to determine when "other grave necessity" may be present to those in parish ministry. Careful education on this question could greatly benefit interchurch families and those who minister to their needs.[20]

Conclusion: A New Paradigm

It can be self-defeating for interchurch families to wring their hands at the tangle of canonists' legal niceties or the shorthand exclusion in worship guidelines. Such temptations abound. But interchurch families alertly seek the dawning light on the horizon of an ecumenically sensitive, reforming church. Theologians need to orient them to its sometimes slow movement. John Hotchkin has served interchurch families well with just such a commentary on Pope John Paul II's December 15, 1981 apostolic exhortation, *Familiaris Consortio,* a document growing out of the 1980 international Synod on the Family.

For one, *Familiaris Consortio* carefully reflects on the marriage of "Christian spouses," "Christian marriage," or "marriage between the baptized." "It does not restrict itself to marriage between Roman Catholic Christians," notes Hotchkin, "but speaks of these along with all Christian marriages, making no demarcation."[21] In the same manner the text (n. 38) "has elevated the question [of 'the promises'] to a new and higher plane," he says. Both spouses are offered a new framework to understand their ministry as the primary religious educators of their children.[22] Moreover, this is the first official document of this character to link "the sacramental life of the family to the ecumenical quest for Christian unity in a direct and positive way."

The text (n. 21) explicitly raises the issues dear to interchurch families: "In particular, participation in the sacrament of reconciliation and in the banquet of the one body of Christ offers to the Christian family the grace and responsibility of overcoming every division and of moving toward the fullness of communion willed by God, responding in this way to the ardent desire of the Lord 'that they may all be one.'" Hotchkin calls attention to n. 59 of the document which emphasizes the family's sharing of the eucharist, where a list of special times to celebrate eucharist follows: births and birthday celebrations, wedding anniversaries of the parents, departures, separations and homecomings, important and far-reaching decisions, and the death of dear ones. "No doubt," writes Hotchkin, "on many of these occasions families, including mixed marriage families, will feel the impulse to shared sacramental action."

Likewise, the text (n. 57) integrates baptism, eucharist and marriage as "intimately connected." Without explicitly attempting new policies for sacramental sharing by interchurch couples, *Familiaris Consortio,* says Hotchkin, "offers a depth of teaching which prompts a restudy and possible revision of those norms [of the Secretariat for Promoting Christian Unity] as they have been thus far elaborated."[23]

Summary

The glacially slow pace of reform in the church seems, at times, imperceptible. Yet in the two decades of development over the issues of ongoing participation in both churches, double belonging, and possibilities for eucharistic sharing for interchurch families which we have explored in this chapter, significant progress has begun. It is in the arena of the religious education and catechesis of interchurch couples and children that the breakthrough remains to be accomplished. The next chapter will undertake to assess this task. For already, signs of creative pastoral initiatives and parental responsibility promise a new stage of interchurch ferment.

Notes

[1]*Foyers Mixtes* 52 (July–September 1981) 33. See also his 1980 article, " 'Double Belonging': Some Reflections," reprinted in *One in Christ* 18 (1982) 31–43, and "L'Oecumenisme dans le Mariage: une Esperance pour l'Eglise," *Etudes* 361 (1984) 387–96.

[2]*L'Osservatore Romano* [English edition] 995:27 (6 July 1987) 5, 10.

[3]Avery Dulles, *The Resilient Church* (Garden City: Doubleday, 1977) 156. His entire chapter 8, "Eucharistic Sharing as an Ecumenical Problem," examines international developments up to 1977. See also George H. Tavard, "Praying Together: *Communicatio in sacris* in the Decree on Ecumenism," in *Vatican II Revisited: By Those Who Were There,* ed. Alberic Stackpoole (Minneapolis: Winston, 1986) 202–19 for a unique historical analysis of the evolution of *UR* 8. Tavard, a peritus at the council, served on the February 1964 drafting session and coined the eventual language for the very phrasing found in the final version (211). He likewise composed Bishop Helmsing's (Kansas City, Missouri) October 4, 1964 relatio formally introducing the text, and describing the *communicatio in sacris* principle as "dialectical." Tavard's careful textual analysis relies heavily on the implications of this dialectic. Moreover, he emphasizes the key adverb *indiscretim,* which is not equivalent to "universally" prohibiting any *communicatio in sacris.* Tavard concludes: "It means that the two aspects of communion (means of grace, and expression of unity) cannot be separated. *Indiscretim* means 'indiscretely' in the sense of 'indiscontinuously,' rather than 'indiscreetly' in the sense of something needing to be done 'with discrimination'" (214).

[4]Dulles, 157–58. Dulles uses the terms intercommunion and eucharistic sharing interchangeably in this section of *The Resilient Church.* However, from the context I think it is clear that he is talking about limited eucharistic sharing.

[5]Ibid. 158.

[6]Ibid. 158–60.

[7]See George Kilcourse, "Ecumenical Marriage: Two Models for Church Unity," *Mid-Stream* 26 (1987) 189–214 for an analysis of French and British developments on eucharistic sharing.

[8]As quoted in Dulles, 163–64.

[9]"Vers l'unité de la communion eucharistique: Instruction pastorale du Synode suisse concernant l'hospitalité eucharistique," *Documentation catholique* 72: 1677 (1975) 529–31.

[10]*Foyers Mixtes* 37–38 (October–December 1977) 98–100.

[11]*Foyers Mixtes* 60 (July–September 1983) 18–20.

[12]Dulles, 165.

[13]*Code of Canon Law: Latin-English Edition* (Washington, DC: Canon Law Society of America, 1983). All references and quotations from the Code will be taken from this edition.

[14]John A. Alesandro, "Pastoral Opportunities," *Chicago Studies* 23 ["The Revised Law of the Church: A Pastoral Guide"] (1984) 97–118.

[15]Cf. J. Cronin, "The Juridical Status of Baptized Non-Catholics in the New Code," *Clergy Review* (1985) 117–128.

[16]Alesandro, 101.

[17]James H. Provost, "Eucharistic Sharing From the Perspective of Roman Catholic Law," *Food for the Journey* (Albuquerque: EDEO-NADEO, 1985) 69–70.

[18]Provost, 70–71.

[19]Provost, 73, 75. For another canon lawyer's helpful interpretation of "mixed marriage" canons in the new Code, see Thomas P. Doyle, "The Roman Catholic Church and Mixed Marriages," *Ecumenical Trends* 14 (1985) 81–84.

[20]James H. Provost, "NCCB Guidelines for Receiving Communion," *Worship* 61 (1987) 223–30.

[21]John F. Hotchkin, "Familiaris Consortio—New Light on Mixed Marriage," *One in Christ* 22 (1986) 75.

[22]Ibid. 77.

[23]Ibid. 78–79.

4. Religious Education and Catechesis

A scene at vacation Bible school found two third-grade girls conversing about the crucifix in the sanctuary of the church where they gathered for daily prayer. The Roman Catholic girl was attempting to explain to the daughter of a Lutheran-Roman Catholic interchurch family that seeing Jesus "still on the cross" helped her to understand how much Jesus had suffered for sins. The interchurch child, who had made her first communion at the Lutheran church, remarked that she preferred the image of a resurrected Jesus in her own parish because they believed Jesus was raised from death. "Well," replied the first girl, "*we* thought of it first!"

Such exchanges remind us how easily children learn religious prejudice and rivalry from parents and other role models. Ecumenists frequently encounter these inherited caricatures, even among the very young. However, this magnifies the potential of sensitive religious educators to eradicate mutual misunderstandings, and to ground a new generation of children in an authentically ecumenical orientation. This chapter will encompass the issues facing interchurch families with the religious education of children. In most instances, the uniquely teachable moments of baptism, first eucharist, and (where applicable) confirmation afford extraordinary opportunities to appreciate the churches' convergence toward full communion. Not only interchurch families but entire parishes can discover the dawning ecumenical horizon in both catechesis for and celebration of these events. An axiom of such catechesis is the realization that parents are the primary religious educators of their children. Given our definition of interchurch couples, the active role of both spouses in preparing children and teenagers for the sacraments becomes a potent ecumenical resource. And the religious identity of interchurch children can manifest the imperfect but certain communion of churches taking progressive steps to restore full communion.

In September 1989 the president and the nation's fifty governors convened in Charlottesville, Virginia for a much heralded "education summit." In the wake of this media event, educators repeated alarms and lamented over the state of our educational systems. (It was reminiscent of the 1983 National Commission on Excellence in Education study, *A Nation at Risk: The Imperative For Educational Reform,* which had lamented the "rising tide of mediocrity" in our schools.) As an illustration, a National Public Radio commentator simultaneously reported that in June 1990 over 700,000 high school students would graduate without being able to read their diplomas. And another 700,000 will have already dropped out of high school this year. The editors of the journal of catechetics, *Living Light,* paraphrased the Charlottesville conference for its readers: "Religious education programs are in crisis." Their diagnosis left little to encourage readers.

A basic overhaul and rethinking of catechetical aims and strategies are needed. Parents, pastors and catechists do not agree on the goals of religious education. Adult programs are unattractive and ineffective. The future of the church is at risk.[1]

We have already called attention to the malpractice and marginalization experienced by too many interchurch families. The mainstream of religious education threatens only to ignore their identity with often mediocre offerings of denominational doctrine, blind to the processes of more effective educational programs, and deaf to the call for positive ecumenical vision. Is it any wonder that "mixed marriages" deteriorate into "baptized unbeliever" families? One conscientious parent asked the question, "It makes you wonder if we're destined to screw up the kids because we're an interchurch couple. Maybe we should discourage other interchurch couples from marrying," he intimated. Very simply put, the challenge that interchurch families present to the churches is twofold: (1) "Will our children have faith?" (2) "Will the churches impede the faith of our children?" The circumference of this chapter can be defined by these questions. We will look in the next chapter, in turn, at interchurch celebrations of baptism, confirmation, and first eucharist. But en route, we will identify some of the underlying issues in terms of future joint religious education programs. By addressing these issues we will fathom how interchurch families articulate deeper ecumenical issues raised by their life and faith.

A Vision of Religious Education

What makes faith mature? That simple question lies at the heart of all religious education efforts. Two recent studies, one a Protestant research project and another a methodic history and analysis by a Roman Catholic scholar, parallel in tracing this central question. The first, *Effective Christian Education: A National Study of Protestant Congregations,*[2] surveyed over 11,000 people in Mainline Protestant and Southern Baptist congregations in the United States. This Lilly-funded research conducted by the Search Institute exposes a flawed religious education system. Two assumptions guided the researchers: (1) rather than reducing faith to adherence to doctrine or dogma, faith is a way of living; (2) faith is life-transforming, having dramatic, lasting impact on believers. The report concludes that many of the factors needed for effective Christian education currently fail to operate in large numbers of the over five hundred congregations studied. The study posits an "integrated" or "mature" faith incorporating both a vertical theme (a life-transforming relationship to a loving God) and a horizontal theme (consistent service to others' needs through acts of love and justice). It is significant that the study does not minimize the potential of religious education programs, but endows them with priority: "Nothing matters more than Christian education." The project director, Peter L. Benson, claimed, "Done well, [religious education] has the potential—more than any other area of congregational life—to promote faith and loyalty."[3] Among key factors that promote faith, the researchers reported, the most important is family religiousness. Family devotions, parents' talking about their faith to children, and family service projects are unrivaled as having the greatest impact on a person's faith.

Mary C. Boys' *Educating in Faith* complements the first study with her review of North American religious education movements in Protestant and Roman Catholic traditions. Her classification of evangelism, religious education, Christian education, and Catholic education facilitates her analysis of historical and theoretical currents across a wide spectrum. What coincides remarkably with *Effective Chris-*

tian Education is her definition: "Religious education is the making accessible of the traditions of the religious community and the making manifest of the intrinsic connection between traditions and transformation."[4] Her concluding chapter, "Movements on the Horizon: Developments and Directions," insists on the very coordinates that define the Search Institute project: religious education involves more than teaching information. The presuppositions of such a reductionistic theory have been discredited by a generation of religious educators who have become interdisciplinary, multilingual in their teaching skills, and insistent on the value of experiential learning and "right brain" activity, which complements the analytical, cognitive, and logical activities of the mind with the person's more intuitive, affective, and non-verbal activities. Boys points to Thomas Groome's emphasis on knowing that encompasses *praxis* as a model: knowing is necessarily "relational, experiential and active." The effect is to invite children, young people, and adults "to make decisions, to respond in faith to what is being taught."[5] In the language of Christian ethics and spirituality, this knowledge is not merely speculative, but evaluative knowledge. Praxis implies that one continually experiences, reflects upon experience, and engages more fully in life with intentionality and reflective knowledge that invests an ethical dimension in our action.

While it is beyond the scope of this chapter to articulate a detailed theory of religious education, I will offer three sources for interchurch families who seek to educate their children in mature Christian faith. The first comes from the theology of conversion as defined by Bernard Lonergan; the second draws from the stages of faith development analyzed by James Fowler; and the third attends to the distinction between individualism and commitment which are central to the research by sociologist of religion Robert Bellah.

Lonergan's Theology of Conversion

Lonergan's transcendental method examines the opportunities for transcendence presented by the dynamism of the human mind itself. By analyzing the possibilities presented by the mind's operations of experiencing (being conscious of data), understanding (explaining the data of experience), judging (applying reason to various understandings, to discern truth or falsity), and deciding (acting on our judgments and values to decide and commit oneself to truth), Lonergan locates a transcendence proper to the human process of coming-to-know. He translates this into four imperatives for the human person: Be attentive! Be intelligent! Be reasonable! Be responsible!

Against this background, Lonergan proceeds in his method to define distinctive types of conversion in terms of a "horizon." The horizon is the "bounding circle," the "limit of one's field of vision." Therefore, a conversion will involve a change of horizon, but not merely a developmental or sequential change of horizon. Conversion involves the repudiation of an old horizon and the about-face turn to a totally new horizon. What lies within this new horizon, as objects of knowledge and interest, is completely new. Such a new beginning or dramatic conversion, for Lonergan, involves the human person in an exercise of freedom that touches the core of one's being, our authenticity as person. The full importance of this conversion process, however, can only be appreciated in the distinctions Lonergan makes between (1) intellectual conversion, (2) moral conversion, and (3) religious conversion.

He defines an *intellectual conversion* as a radical clarification, and consequently the elimination of an exceedingly stubborn and misleading myth concerning reality, objectivity and human knowledge. The classroom has traditionally been the arena for such intellectual conversions. When we learn economics, how money can work for us, this clarification eliminates the piggy-bank concept of saving money. In medical school, physicians learn how various therapies and drugs can alleviate symptoms, or how surgical procedures can eliminate sources of dysfunction in various diseased or damaged organs. Similarly, Lonergan's own definition of the various conversions invites an intellectual conversion because he clarifies three distinct and different conversions.

A *moral conversion* involves the change in the criterion of one's decisions and choices. Here we see the operations of the human mind engaged at higher and higher levels: deciding. By committing oneself to truth, the claims of truth on our person magnify. (This is Thomas Groome's point in his emphasis on praxis, discussed above.) For example, when a child begins to change the criterion of decisions from self-satisfaction to a response to the needs of others to be satisfied, a moral conversion happens. We migrate through an autobiography of reigning values that define who we are at particular moments. On the other hand, Lonergan's conversion process permits a regression—the Yuppie who reverts to self-satisfaction, abandoning the virtues of justice or the dignity of human persons in favor of corporate career-climbing. How we decide on what values or virtues to pursue is the ethical task. In a complex world we face rival theories: ranging from the utilitarian claim (the greatest good for the greatest number determines the morally good) to the deontological claim (certain actions of their very nature, e.g. abortion, are absolutely morally evil).

Finally, a *religious conversion* means to be grasped by an ultimate concern; it is the total transformation of the human person, entailing the total and permanent self-surrender to a new basis for valuing and doing good. For Lonergan, religious conversion is a dynamic state. In Christianity it means the experience of God's love flooding our hearts through the Holy Spirit given to us; it is the experience of God's grace, the totally unmerited experience of God's loving presence in Christ, and our transformation as persons in God's loving presence. God's love, then, becomes the ground of our own self-transcendence, the very basis for our own valuing and action. Religious education which situates intellectual and moral conversions vis-à-vis the primacy of religious conversion will not neglect these traditional emphases, but appreciate them from a new perspective. Imagine the interchurch couple reflecting with children on their experience of falling-in-love as spouses, narrated as a religious conversion!

Theologians subsequent to Lonergan have accordingly refined his sense of an *affective conversion,* that the human person was "self-transcendent affectively when he fell in love, when the isolation of the individual was broken and he spontaneously functioned not just for himself but for others as well."[6] In this sense, we not only know and value, but we *desire* the other(s) for the sake of the goodness of the other(s), and we seek to enhance his or her (their) being. The beauty of this Christian phenomenology of human love remains that in mutuality we ourselves become transformed. Perhaps the greatest insight Lonergan affords interchurch families is that a religious education that defines conversion as a one-dimensional experience, or that confuses intellectual or moral conversion with the completeness of religious conversion as other-worldly falling-in-love, risks eclipsing the involving, autobiographical emphases which offer maps for the new directions we have appropriated from the bellwether studies, *Educating for Faith* and *Effective Christian Education.*

Fowler's Stages of Faith

James Fowler's cognitive-developmental theory of stages of faith[7] alerts us to similar emphases. His seven stages have limitations, particularly insofar as they are "structures" or "operations of knowing and valuing," which tell us nothing about the content of faith at various stages. Nonetheless, *primal faith* tells us something about bonding and trust of the infant for parents. At the pre-school age (2–5) an *intuitive-projective faith* reveals a qualitatively new self that uses language and imagination to locate meaning. The following stage of *mythic-literal* faith (6–10) accelerates the child's reliance on narrative, on stories as the reservoir of implicit values and a family's community of meanings and mutuality, reciprocity. Fowler finds most Americans in the fourth stage which is appropriate to the development of adolescents (11–20), a *synthetic-conventional faith* where a new self-consciousness and interiority competes with a purely "tacit" synthesis of beliefs and values. Progress to *individuative-reflective faith* comes for maturing persons in their twenties, when the executive ego's self-reflections lead to an explicit commitment and accountability, a critical choice of beliefs, values, and commitments. The enviable final two stages are particularly important for interchurch families and ecumenists. At the *conjunctive faith* stage (mid-life) one acknowledges paradoxes with a humbling awareness that truth is more complex than once admitted; there is an openness to traditions outside one's own; a "second naiveté" returns to the symbols of the religious myths and finds more than a now-abandoned first literalism. The final stage, *universalizing faith,* affords the perspective of the love of the creator for all creation as the basis for valuing all life. This expansive perspective resonates with Mary Boys' meta-

phor of a less constricted model of religious education,
"dilating our sense of the world."[8] Without lingering on
Fowler's theory, it is important to remark that the same
experiential, autobiographical, narrative sources of theology identified in his stages lead to the fuller ethic of interpersonal responsibility and compassionate love as found in
Lonergan's method. Efforts at religious education which
appropriate Fowler's insights can more adequately engage
interchurch families by emphasizing the role of biblical
narratives. They can also incorporate the experiences of
interchurch families who already live progressive steps
toward full communion of the churches as an illustration of
the highest levels of faith development.

Bellah's Critique of Individualism

Finally, Robert Bellah's research in the past decade
rounds out our sources for educating children in mature
Christian faith. While Bellah's work has been less directly
integrated in religious education circles, it accents even
more distinctly the trajectory from a personal faith to
a social ethic—*Effective Christian Education's* horizontal
theme, and *Education for Mature Faith's* attention to praxis as
interpersonal, experiential, and active. Bellah and the co-
authors of *Habits of the Heart*[9] identify three historic strands
in the American culture: the biblical, the republican, and
individualism. This study cautions that the first two strands
are in danger of being eclipsed by excesses in forms of
American individualism.

The biblical strand, richly cultivated by the founders of
America, promoted as its goal the just and compassionate
society. Success was measured not in material terms but as
the creation of a community with a genuinely ethical and
spiritual life. Freedom meant the liberty to do that which is

good, just and honest. Justice, Bellah emphasizes, is not merely procedural but substantive. The values of the biblical narrative (community, covenant, justice and human dignity) are paralleled in the Jeffersonian vision of the *res publica,* or "public things," that the political life of a community or nation protects and advances. The republican strand of American culture promoted as its goal the ideals of citizenship and participatory democracy. There was a fundamental political equality. When the pursuit of money displaced active civic participation, tyranny resulted.

The historical matrix out of which American individualism emerged owed much to the philosophical shift to a subjective emphasis. Bellah identifies two such expressions in American history. *Utilitarian individualism,* personified by Benjamin Franklin's frugality and thrift, promoted as its goal the amassing of wealth and power for the self via competitive enterprise. The disadvantages of its vision were the loss of a larger social context and responsibility (a form of Social Darwinism, or economic survival of the fittest). From poet Walt Whitman emerged *expressive individualism,* which promoted the goal of freedom to express oneself. While this led to a life rich with experiences and open to diverse peoples, its "downside" was a drift toward exaggerations in sensuality, intellectual pursuits, and strong feelings. What recommends this study is the two hundred interviews which give it a narrative tenor. The most useful chapter is an analysis of "Religion" which locates most Americans as "mystics" on Ernst Troeltsch's spectrum of church-sect-mysticism. This proves particularly revealing as Bellah remarks that once religion in the United States became "dis-established," it was, in effect, privatized. The loss of biblical and republican strands becomes more evident in this profile of the majority of Americans who practice their own form of mysticism while juxtaposed in church pews every Sunday. The potential of the churches as "communities of memory" to empower mature faith is lost. The communal expression of Christianity suffers, becoming what one pundit has dubbed "Christianity lite," or without the social ethic that influences public policy.[10] While an ambitious study for interchurch families, anyone concerned with religious education that integrates a fuller ethic of mature faith in personal and social responsibility would profit from Bellah's diagnosis of individualism's plague of the American psyche and spirit. It is ironic that so much religious education that presupposed an individualized (read, privatized) approach to religious education manifests the very malaise of utilitarian and expressive forms of individualism. Mary Boys has summed up nicely this dilemma: "Since the Enlightenment Western society has tended to confuse technological advance with progress, information with knowledge, reason with wisdom, credentials with education, and teaching with technique."[11]

An Identity for Interchurch Children

A five year old boy, the son of an Episcopal mother and a Roman Catholic father, asked: "Mommy, this Sunday are we going to the 'Ay-men' church or the 'Ah-men' church?" In that vignette we recognize a child's ability to perceive differences—but also the child's experience as a witness that our differences need not be divisive. We are entering the second generation of interchurch children as interchurch family young adults marry one another. The British Association of Interchurch Families points out that children's adaptable nature facilitates interchurch identity during the formative years. "Variation in the form of church worship, far from confusing the child, does in fact sharpen their interest in what it is all about and increases awareness of the meaningfulness, or otherwise, of prayer." They go on to emphasize that children "do not attach a denominational label. It is all 'family churchgoing.'"[12]

Interchurch families demonstrate an uncanny ability to rise above denominationalism. We discussed their identity in Chapter 1, under René Beaupère's suggested "double belonging" thesis. While some discredit this attempt, the reality of a bond of communion by virtue of a common baptism, and, in interchurch couples' cases, of the sacramental reality of marriage, retrieves our discussion of progressive stages toward *full communion.* The ability and desire of interchurch families to rise above denominationalism must not be interpreted as religious indifference. These couples and children strive for fidelity to the two churches. Indifference only leads to a non-religious marriage, a family whose religious identity has been neutralized. A poignant episode of such indifference was recalled by a mother who at one point chose not to attend any church. Her young son innocently asked her one day, "Mommy, don't you like God?" Interchurch families actually intensify their children's appreciation of mature Christian faith.

A 1986 *Time* magazine report on "modeling" in American families dramatically portrayed the impact of parental faith or indifference on children. While not addressing interchurch couples' "modeling," the implications are evident, perhaps more strikingly significant for interchurch children. If *both* parents regularly attend church with their children, 77% of their children will remain faithful in church attendance as adults. If only the *father* attends church with his children, 55% of those children will remain faithful. If only the *mother* attends with her children, only 25% of the children will remain faithful. If *neither parent* attends, only 6% will be faithful adults.

Children negotiate a wide spectrum of family diversity. They ordinarily have two sets of grandparents (complicated in today's culture with second marriages and sometimes as many as four sets of grandparents). They perceive profound differences—economic, social, geographic, lifestyle—yet develop healthy relationships despite the wide spectrum. No one clamors for restricting marriage in order to minimize these differences, lest the children not have a clear, univocal identity in their extended families. Just as the American experience often has integrated a diverse ethnic identity—Irish married Italians, French married Germans, Eastern Europeans married Hispanics in the second generation of immigrant families during the past century—so, too, children have emerged healthy and with an enriched identity, celebrating ethnic heritages and customs. Advice about the marriage having no chance of surviving or the children being confused beyond imagination became legendary. Many of us trace our family tree, only to find that we have succeeded where prophets of gloom thundered dismal prospects. The analogy with the experience of interchurch families bears careful scrutiny.

One interchurch couple recollected their daughter's awakening to the question of her religious identity at the age of five. They confessed that they did not realize their doctrinal differences or conflicts until their child's questions began to surface. Their immediate responses, they realized, were contradictory. The Roman Catholic father was inclined to give a concrete answer—with the hope, he added, that she would outgrow this stage of literalism. The mother, an Episcopalian, on the other hand was reluctant, she admitted, to give any concrete or technical answers. In retrospect the couple has come to a wisdom about a deeper dynamic beyond either extreme. Just as parents honestly and yet with a precise measure answer a five year old's question about human sexuality, so they answer questions about faith, church, and religion. Would you really give a five year old a medical manual or sex therapy guide when he or she asks where babies come from? Why give them the *Baltimore Catechism* when they ask about God's love or Jesus' healing the sick? Again, the British AIF cautions that "avoiding friction by keeping silent on matters of religion is not helpful to the children." What children do experience is their parents' attitudes toward religion—whether it is a source of tension and disunity, or a sharing of common essentials of faith with ecumenical hope and energy to cope with reconciling what divides and keeps us apart. Children can even manipulate perceived friction in religious issues to their own advantage, a reflex often only uncoiled in the adolescent years. Reflecting a knowledge of contemporary child development theories and psychology, interchurch couples are reminded what a precious opportunity for consciousness-raising (their identity as members of a family of churches, rather than competing denominations) early childhood offers.

It is not till the age of 11–12 onwards that children begin to develop the thinking ability to be able to express mystery in abstract terms. Hence in all religious teaching it is important not to give them theological words before they have the intellectual or spiritual equipment to deal with them. Such teaching rings no bell in their experience, and often leads to misconceptions that remain into adult life, if no chance is given to them to discover or express in other terms what the mysteries of faith mean. For the child of an interchurch couple the confusions that could arise from being exposed to differences of belief in two traditions are more serious, when the beliefs are expressed in theological language he is not able to understand. Fr. Anthony Bullen's advice is helpful. Don't worry if you cannot give a full answer to some

of your child's questions. "How is Jesus in the host?"
The answer is, quite simply, "We don't know. We just
know that he is."[13]

One interchurch parent, Brian J. McNulty, has signaled
a common discovery by couples "that exposure to each
other's traditions has overcome fear and misunderstanding
of those traditions."[14] That makes possible the involvement
with another tradition while claiming a commitment with
one's own tradition. His description of it not always being
easy "to live 'between the lines'" captures the experience of
many families. Overcoming fears and misconceptions
about each other's church takes effort. Without such an
intentional motive, interchurch families are threatened to
become dysfunctional families. Most of the literature on
such family dysfunction gravitates to emotional disorders
and chemical dependencies as the sources of upheaval. The
long-range toll exacted from children and spouses robs persons of healthy physical and spiritual well-being. What is
only beginning to be examined are the ways in which the
diverse churches live as a dysfunctional family. What price
do we as Christians pay for the less than desirable ecumenical health of our churches?

While we addressed some of the demographics of de-
clining Mainline Protestant churches in Chapter 1, recent
research funded by the Lilly Foundation has detailed new
developments.[15] Why are baby boomers staying away from
the churches? Does interchurch marriage mean the search
for a third denomination? How has the liberal-conservative
split within the Protestant denominations polarized, and
thus jeopardized, the future of the churches? One way of describing these phenomena vis-à-vis the spectrum of interchurch marriages is to assess the cutting-edge research of the
American south as a laboratory for a new interchurch fu-

ture. Louis McNeil[16] of the Glenmary Research Center in Atlanta has effectively contrasted the cultural-religious context of the American south with ecumenical models from previous generations emerging from the American north. The Catholic Church, he reports, succeeded in moderating northern Protestantism by the sheer size of its membership. Ecumenical relations between Catholics and Protestants in the northern United States have tended to be comfortable, even cozy. Dean Kelley's 1972 classic, *Why Conservative Churches Are Growing,*[17] is singled out by McNeil as a reliable taxonomy, contrasting churches in terms of categories such as strictness/leniency, and exclusivist/ecumenical. In these terms, Catholicism as a strong religion achieved a public role and muted major characteristics of Evangelical Protestantism in the north.

Because Evangelicalism has thrived in the south, a new situation has developed. McNeil suggests that it will be the harbinger of a new ecumenical configuration, one in which Catholics will be a minority. American Evangelicalism is characterized by five traits: (1) evangelical/biblical; (2) democratic/egalitarian; (3) voluntary; (4) congregational; (5) personal. This contrasts with Catholicism's traits: (1) ecclesial/sacramental; (2) hierarchical; (3) cultural/familial and socially rooted; (4) episcopal; (5) institutional or ecclesial-mediation. The question that looms large for Catholics will be whether Catholicism can adapt creatively, or inculturate itself in the context of Evangelicalism's dominant public role in the south. If not, then Catholicism in the south is threatened with further erosion, even resembling the more socially constricted profile of the Episcopal Church outside that tradition's historic centers such as New England.

McNeil's use of Kelley's dichotomy, strong vs. lenient religion, interprets the dilemma of Catholics in the south.

The "strong" religion manifests: (1) commitment; (2) missionary zeal; (3) discipline; (4) certainty; (5) conformity; (6) passion. The "lenient" religion exhibits: (1) cognizance of relative values; (2) pluralism; (3) dialogue; (4) passivity; (5) individuality; (6) reserve. Tension in an Evangelical-Roman Catholic interchurch marriage comes when the Evangelical spouse "prevail[s] with the children, or civic community, without the 'lenient' [Catholic] partner having done little more than appease, leaving depths cf feeling unchanged, perhaps even exacerbated." In McNeil's analysis, these hidden sources of "miscommunication" in Evangelical-Catholic marriages in the south deserve careful pastoral care.

> Not only is there cause for a great deal of tension in marriages between partners of "strong" and "lenient" traditions, but the nature of the tensions may well be mislabelled. Disagreement on child-rearing; family prayer styles; social networking with friends; economic activity etc. may all have their roots in religious values while the flash point of disagreement may center on personalities (friends); temperament (prayer); strategy (child-rearing); drive, energy, or ambition (economic activity and preferences).[18]

Some might argue that Catholicism is now migrating in a neo-conservative direction that moves it back toward a "strong" religion category. However, in the south such a shift would mean further isolation of Catholics, a decided minority. What Evangelical-Catholic interchurch families in the south are negotiating could well presage new patterns and pastoral questions as the so-called "southernization" of the United States unfolds. The consolidation of parishes in strong Catholic centers like Detroit and Chicago presents symptoms of dissolution. Will the identity of interchurch family children more and more gravitate toward the Evangelical tradition when parochial school systems consolidate or diminish? When juxtaposed with the growth of Evangelical and Conservative churches around the country, McNeil's probing questions suggest new motives to address the growing importance of pastoral care of mixed marriages and interchurch family identity.

Summary

We began this chapter by delineating a vision of religious education. Mature religious faith, we saw, involves parents as the primary religious educators of children. For interchurch families this affords unique ecumenical experiences to integrate into a child's ongoing intellectual, moral, affective, and religious conversions, and stages of faith development. The experiences of community available to an interchurch child provide a potent antidote to the cultural lures of individualism. Moreover, those experiences within an interchurch family can be life-transforming for children, as well as for the community in which their catechetical and sacramental initiation is celebrated.

The question of an identity for interchurch children need not be problematic or a negative factor, but a conversion experience which is genuinely revelatory of the ecumenical future for parents, children, and the entire community of faith.

The future catechesis of interchurch and other children promises to reflect both the doctrinal consensus of reuniting churches and ongoing experiences in the reconciliation process between individual Christians and their churches. Because the summit of the church's life is liturgy celebrated by the gathered community, we turn next to the powerful symbolic potential of interchurch families' experience of the sacraments to animate and challenge a fuller understanding of identity and mission.

Notes

[1]"Editor's Foreword: A Religious Education Summit?" *Living Light* 26:1 (Fall 1989) 3.

[2]Peter Benson and Carolyn H. Eklin, *Effective Christian Education: A National Study of Protestant Congregations—A Summary Report on Faith, Loyalty, and Congregational Life* (Minneapolis: Search Institute, 1990).

[3]Eugene C. Roehlkepartain, "What Makes Faith Mature?" *Christian Century* 107 (May 9, 1990) 496–99.

[4]Mary C. Boys, *Educating in Faith* (San Francisco: Harper & Row, 1989) 193.

[5]Ibid. 158. Cf. Thomas Groome, *Christian Religious Education: Sharing Our Story and Vision* (San Francisco: Harper & Row, 1980).

[6]Bernard Lonergan, *Method in Theology* (New York: The Seabury Press, 1972) 289.

[7]*Becoming Adult, Becoming Christian* (San Francisco: Harper & Row, 1984).

[8]Boys, 154.

[9]*Habits of the Heart: Individualism and Commitment in American Life* (San Francisco: Harper & Row, 1985).

[10]Cf. Richard P. McBrien, *Caesar's Coin: Religion and Politics in America* (New York: Macmillan, 1987), offers a formidable historical and legal study of the American experiment, emphasizing the contribution of John Courtney Murray, with a case study of the 1984 presidential campaign and issues engaged with church and politics in that event. For a classic Protestant study, see Martin E. Marty, *The Public Church: Mainline-Evangelical-Catholic* (New York: Crossroad, 1981).

[11]Boys, 154.

[12]*Two-Church Families* (2nd ed.; Sussex, England: AIF, 1983) 32. See also the Rev. Dr. Gregory C. Wingenbach, *Two . . . Yet One In*

Christ (Brookline: [Greek Orthodox] Department of Church and Family Life, 1989), for an excellent contribution of interchurch and intercultural pastoral care in the Greek Orthodox context. Cf. Aidan Kavanagh, *Elements of Rite* (New York: Pueblo Publishing Co., 1982) 67–68, wherein he addresses the fact of disenfranchising infants and children from the liturgy. He likewise cautions: "Children may well be early and forceful witnesses to liturgical atrophy in their assembly, and . . . their witness should be taken seriously by all. Children learn much by vigorous ritual engagement. . . . They learn perhaps even more by observing what ritual and liturgy do to adults, especially their parents, and to their peers and siblings."

[13]*Two-Church Families,* 32.

[14]"Ecumenical Children," *Atonement* (April 1988) 1–2. This reflection was written as a response to Carol Eipers, "Will Our Children Be Ecumenical?" *Atonement* (February–March 1988).

[15]John C. Long (ed.), "Rough Waters for Mainstream Protestant Churches," *Progressions* 2:1 (January 1990).

[16]Louis McNeill, paper presented to NADEO Research and Development Committee, Atlanta, February 3, 1990.

[17]*Why Conservative Churches Are Growing: A Study in Sociology of Religion* (New York: Harper & Row, 1972) and a 1986 reprint with a new introduction by Mercer University Press.

[18]McNeil, 3.

5. Sacraments and Interchurch Families

A boy on the verge of his first communion queried his mother about his catechesis. "Don't they teach us that Jesus invites us to the table?" he asked. "And isn't the eucharist Jesus' way of bringing us to unity as a family of faith? Then why won't they let my daddy receive at my first communion?" Such interchurch children's questions disarm us and demand careful pastoral consideration of the needs and gifts they personify.

Nowhere does the experience of an interchurch family ask more of the churches' ecumenical resolve than in the celebration of sacraments for interchurch children. And how the local church and parish respond to the gifts and needs of interchurch families plays the decisive role in their ongoing belonging to, or exodus from, the church. Veteran interchurch couples generally recommend anticipating questions such as: In what church will our child be baptized? Celebrate first communion? Be confirmed? Continue religious education? Some recommend resolving these and other questions even before the marriage is sacramentally celebrated. But an increasing majority of interchurch couples recommend making such decisions from *within the process* of their own evolving identity as an interchurch couple. The past generation's solutions (e.g. daughters will be baptized and raised in the mother's church; sons, in the father's) no longer satisfy couples who seek to enrich and to integrate their children's faith with both traditions (double belonging).

What follows should not be misconstrued as a "how-to" guide for families seeking easy answers. Because these issues and questions emerge from the pastoral arena, they admit of no recipes or cut-and-dried resolution. Our second chapter focused some of the underlying principles of ecumenism that empower interchurch families to request intelligently (yes, at times tenaciously) that these needs be pastorally addressed. We find here the dynamics of the churches' "certain, if imperfect" unity (*UR,* 3). Our discussion of the sacraments and interchurch children advocates nothing less than the possibilities envisioned and already set in motion by the Second Vatican Council and parallel ecclesial commitments in other traditions. Because the United States affords virtually no formal models or guidelines for the sacraments and interchurch children, many of the suggestions that follow rely on the British Association of Interchurch Families and French *Foyers Mixtes* publications. The suggestions are offered here in the hope of provoking a dialogue with American interchurch families and pastoral ministers.

Baptism

The full impact of existing obstacles to church unity usually avalanches an interchurch couple on the occasion of the baptism of their first child. While the churches ordinarily mutually recognize one another's baptism (with the major exception of the "believer's [adult] baptism" vs. infant baptism debate), the complete process of Christian Initiation must be considered as the context for the churches' dialogue. In this sense, the 1982 study of the Joint Committee of the Episcopal Diocesan Ecumenical Officers (EDEO) and the National Association of Diocesan Ecumenical Officers (NADEO), *ARC Baptisms,*[1] provides a model of insight. This Episcopal-Roman Catholic study begins with the premise that there is no such event as an "ecumenical baptism." Baptism of its very nature signifies an ecumenical reality. What interchurch couples and their churches can achieve is a *fuller expression* of this ecumenical dimension. Baptism places the newly baptized (and every baptized person who renews the baptismal covenant on these occasions) in a unique relationship with all baptized persons—past, present, and future.

By inviting members of their parishes and congregations to gather for the baptismal liturgy, interchurch couples and pastors can make visible this common baptism as a sacrament of unity. What the couple must avoid at all costs is an impression or feeling that a wedge has been driven into their marriage and family by the baptism of their child. At this moment they together reaffirm their identity as an interchurch family of faith (just as in the marriage liturgy) and a joint role in the child's religious education. They help the gathered community to understand the divisions of the churches without accepting or tolerating them. Here is manifest the gift of an interchurch couple as the conscience and catalyst of Christian unity.

The experience of one young interchurch couple who began to explore the possibilities for baptizing their new baby illustrates well the pitfalls, but eventual joy, negotiated in such a celebration. Jim, the Roman Catholic father, was an enviable parishioner, having recently completed a term as parish council chair. Jenny, the Methodist mother, regularly volunteered in her congregation's educational programs and communications committee publications. Both participated in the other church's worship and social life. When Jim approached his pastor to inquire about their daughter's baptism, expressing the hope that their interchurch identity might be signaled as a gift for the churches, the pastor discouraged him with the explanation that "we do baptisms once a month at the Sunday liturgy, and you come to a preparation class a few weeks prior."

After intimating his discouragement to Jenny, they approached the Methodist pastor who appreciated their request and was more than willing to celebrate the baptism with emphasis on a common baptism and the commitment of the couple to their interchurch identity. In the intervening weeks, overtures to the Catholic pastor on the part of another priest raised his consciousness. Eventually he wrote a letter which was read at the Methodist church on the Sunday of the baptism, remarking our common baptism and reaffirming the commitment of the parish to continue working toward the Second Vatican Council's pledge to the restoration of full communion. He affirmed Jim and Jenny in their interchurch identity. Godparents included a Catholic and a Methodist. Both sets of grandparents gathered in the sanctuary for the baptism. And friends from Jim's parish presented a certificate from the neighborhood community ministries' organization, a twenty-six church covenant, that affirmed the mutual recognition of baptism by all the neighboring churches.

In 1980 the British AIF wrote to the Synod of Bishops of the deep distress that can affect a marriage when baptism is celebrated by the church of one partner, to the exclusion of the other: "The interchurch couple need to know that their child is accepted by both their Churches; they need to experience that they themselves are accepted by both their Churches; they need to receive the blessing and encouragement of both their Churches in what they are trying to do in their marriage and in their family."[2] AIF emphasized the admirable decision of interchurch couples to celebrate baptism into the one church of Christ as it exists within the present divided churches of mother and father. This avoids the neglect or indifference practiced in some circles where baptism and religious education are deferred until the child or adolescent can express a preference.

French *Foyers Mixtes* articles chronicle projects to promote more ecumenically responsive celebrations of baptism by interchurch couples as early as 1968. The 1972 "Common Declaration on Baptism"[3] prepared by the French Catholic-Protestant committee underscored the *one* baptism shared by members of separated churches. "If the single baptism introduces us into the communion of the Body of Christ," stated the text, "we are called to advance toward a deeper communion in looking for ways to express visibly that which we have already been given and to witness together our common hope." René Beaupère commented on one of numerous descriptions of "ecumenical baptisms," this event being on the occasion of the twenty-fifth anniversary of the Ecumenical Council of Churches in Geneva. Writing in 1973, Beaupère suggested the couple had misplaced the problem by turning to the ecumenical meeting. The solemn cathedral worship of the council, he remarked, could not be the place where the "ecumenical baptism" takes place. "The ecumenical council is not able, as such, to celebrate the sacraments: it is not a church, but a simple organ of dialogue and collaboration between Christian communities." The ecclesiological question posed by baptism, Beaupère underlined, is one of the *communion* of all those who confess Jesus Christ as savior.[4] The nemesis of interchurch families, the charge of creating a "third church," is adroitly avoided by Beaupère's careful theological reflection. The sacramental events are celebrations of the parish, the local, identifiable parochial (or congregational) community of a particular confession. To speak of baptism in an "ecumenical environment" risks the possibility that a family, such as this Geneva example, might refuse to insert itself in the communities from which it came.

From 1975 onward, *Foyers Mixtes* articles report the more frequent practice of dual registration of baptisms in the churches of both the wife and husband in an interchurch marriage. The rationale behind this formality recommends it as a mutual recognition of baptism. Canonists have raised questions, particularly in the Roman Catholic Church, about the permission for pastors to meet this request. It is helpful to remark that marriages involving a Catholic and spouse from another church, when celebrated in the other church and witnessed by the minister, are recorded in Catholic marriage registers. Are there analogies here that might promote this pastoral practice? Could it be an interim step in recognizing a sense of "double belonging" by interchurch children? Ecumenists and interchurch couples have begun to ask if a definitive confessional identity is, in fact, necessarily chosen with the particular church in which the baptism is celebrated.

Following the remarkable 1982 convergence statement of the Faith and Order Commission of the World Council of Churches, *Baptism, Eucharist and Ministry,* readers of *Foyers Mixtes* reflected on the event of a baptism of three infants which was planned in the light of *BEM* reflections. Steps and progress toward the celebration at a Roman Catholic Sunday eucharist were described by two interchurch couples, one with an eighteen month old daughter, and one with two sons, eighteen months old and two months old. Interestingly, "careful of the balance," the Reformed woman pastor baptized two children, one from each family; the Catholic priest baptized the oldest son of the second family. Eucharistic hospitality was extended to all. The couple concluded by remarking "the impact of such a ceremony on the community."[5] Such descriptions may stretch some pastors and members of the community beyond their limits. Yet the attempt to maintain the integrity of the distinct traditions, and efforts to implement possibilities for joint worship, deserve intelligent and constructive criticism. The widely publicized celebration of Pentecost 1989 baptism by Bishop Francis Quinn of Sacramento, California and his Episcopal, Lutheran, and Orthodox peer-bishops stands as a prophetic ecumenical action, independent of the interchurch family identity. Each bishop baptized his own infant-candidates in a common liturgy. Yet the application of this principle of a common baptism to the gifts and needs of interchurch families draws us further into the drama of Christian Initiation. In the words of an interchurch husband, theologian Geoffrey Wainwright, the ethical horizon of our baptismal promises commits us to heal the world's divisions and injustices: "I suspect, however, that the sacraments will eventually be revalued, now that the days of 'cheap grace' are over," he has conjectured. "It is socially and culturally a costly act to receive baptism in the German Democratic Republic. . . ."[6]

First Eucharist

The seven year old daughter of a Presbyterian-Roman Catholic interchurch couple attended a parochial school. Her parents had decided that the resources of the parish school would better meet their educational expectations. In the course of her first two years in school, they discussed whether she would celebrate first communion with her second-grade classmates. It was agreed, with the Presbyterian mother quite comfortable with their decision. One project that occupied them in the weeks before the event was the purchase of a first communion dress. After numerous shopping trips, one was chosen. On the Sunday morning as the interchurch couple arrived at the parish with their daughter, her Presbyterian mother gasped when she looked inside the child's classroom. Her daughter was the only child wearing a flowered, pastel dress! To her credit, the daughter was unflappable. In fact, the pretty dress was the envy of other mothers and all of the girls who were decked in white dresses.

Such customs which are taken for granted in various church traditions often surprise and humiliate interchurch families. The kaleidoscope of distinctive ethos, unspoken and deep in the marrow of our corporate church identities, affords a rich diversity in our unity as Christians. It must always be appreciated, but not placed as an impediment to the path toward full communion.

Religious educators report that it is only on the occasion of first communion catechesis that many interchurch families are recognized in their uniqueness. In a highly mobile society, many children begin school in a parish, neighborhood, or even a city different from their birth and baptism locale. The question of sacraments and belonging to the church actually precipitate in the event of first communion. Some pastoral ministers have discovered that interchurch families are involved in their programs only after several sessions of sacramental preparation with parents. How often is the catechesis attentive to the issues of common baptism? How frequently is the catechesis on eucharist addressed to the process of restoring full communion between divided churches? To what extent are interchurch parents advised about possibilities for eucharistic sharing?

The experience of the British AIF concerning first communion was summarized in a 1981 article that insisted that the choice for this event "cannot be made in a vacuum: it does not come upon the parents out of the blue and cannot be sprung suddenly upon the child. Rather it is a choice that will grow out of all the other choices the parents have successively made: about baptism; about family practice of public worship; about schooling."[7] Their 1980 conference on Christian education and interchurch families repeated the right and obligation of the parents to exercise directly their responsibility in preparing children for first communion. AIF has consistently appealed to the churches for both parents, who together brought the child to this point of maturing faith, to receive communion with the child. A subsequent article on "Eucharistic Sharing in Interchurch Families" trenchantly marked the pastoral issue:

> A study of actual eucharistic practice in the different age groups makes it possible to trace a progressive development within the experience of marriage and parenthood. It is clear that many older couples who accepted—and albeit reluctantly—at the time of their marriage and baptism of the children that they could not receive communion together, have come to feel impelled—in the absence of authorisation—to accept responsibility themselves for unofficial eucharistic sharing as their children come to communicant status. The crisis point which impels them to make this decision often comes when a child is prepared to take first communion. The strain of separation at communion between husband and wife as mature adults may just be tolerable. It often appears intolerable to set this bad and unintelligible example to young children as they begin their communicant life.[8]

In French circles the first communion question surfaces just as in the British AIF in the context of eucharistic sharing policies. The related question of "At what age first communion?" has preoccupied much *Foyers Mixtes* discussion because the Reformed Church has traditionally delayed first communion until the age of fourteen or fifteen. The modern Roman Catholic custom (following Pope Pius X's reforms), recommending first communion at six or seven years of age, has provided an opportune convergence as the Reformed churches changed pastoral practice to recommend more frequent eucharistic celebrations and full participation in the Lord's supper at younger ages.

René Beaupère rehearsed the ferment in theological circles over the process of Christian initiation (with an emphasis on eucharist) in a moving pastoral letter to a perplexed mother. He has noted the use of the phrases "profession of faith" and "feasts of faith" associated with both first communion and confirmation to underscore the renewal of foundational baptismal promises in all three sacraments. Beaupère has suggested that the respective Catholic and Protestant catechetical processes are not "parallel" in the sense that two parallel lines never meet. He boldly posed the ecclesiological question in remarking that the churches reunite at many points: ecumenical celebrations of baptism; interchurch catechesis. He has concluded: "First Communion no longer forces the definitive choice of one church in opposition to the other."[9] When seen in the context of our Chapter 2 discussion about eucharistic sharing, the new possibilities for celebrating first communion for interchurch children reverses the trauma of this event as a divisive experience for interchurch families. One could make a convincing case that the need for eucharist by the interchurch family, and the nature of this unique event of first communion, could qualify them to appeal to canon 844 of the Roman Catholic Church's 1983 revised *Code of Canon Law* which provides for possibilities of eucharistic sharing.

The eucharist is ultimately the sacrament of the body of Christ. This implies that those who celebrate it express and receive their identity as body of Christ in the world. In the language of *Baptism, Eucharist and Ministry* the transforming effects of the eucharist extend the ethical conversion which lies at the heart of our vision of religious education: "The eucharistic celebration demands reconciliation and sharing . . . and is a constant challenge in the search for appropriate relationships in social, economic, and political life. All kinds of injustice, racism, separation and lack of freedom are radically challenged when we share in the body and blood of Christ" (n. 20).

Confirmation

The sacrament of confirmation has been described as a rite in search of a rationale. The history of the dissolution of the threefold rite of Christian initiation (baptism-confirmation-eucharist) evidences the loss of theological moorings for confirmation as practiced by the church today.[10] Questions of "What age for confirmation?" invariably distract religious educators, pastoral ministers, and parents from the larger context of the process of Christian initiation and the full communion experienced in baptism, eucharist, and confirmation. In this sense, confirmation ultimately speaks about the mature faith which characterizes the vision of religious education analyzed in the previous chapter.

Unlike baptism, interchurch experience of confirmation is virtually non-existent. However, the attitude that confirmation makes a person once and for all a member of one particular denomination, sealing forever the status quo of divided churches, invariably damages interchurch families whose gifts and needs are neglected in this sacrament. The British AIF groups repeatedly decry the rite of confirmation to "seal" denominational loyalty in an exclusivist, anti-ecumenical manner. When celebrated in relationship to baptism, eucharist, and the fuller process of entry into the church, the body of Christ, this mature commitment in faith must promote the quest for unity so precious to interchurch families. Joseph Laishley has written about the confusion of the churches over the meaning of confirmation. "If confirmation is to be seen as in some significant sense the 'seal of the Spirit,' then it can have no divisive meaning," he reminded in a 1981 British AIF article. "The Spirit will have no part in division."[11]

Some interchurch families have posed the question: Why not record interchurch family confirmations in the registry of both churches, as in baptism? In 1980 Roman Catholic and Anglican bishops in Telford, England celebrated a joint confirmation liturgy. The rite was composed of the essential elements from both churches, with the simultaneous confirmation of candidates by the bishops who laid hands and anointed their respective candidates. The Anglicans even adopted the Catholic custom requiring sponsors to present candidates individually to the bishop.[12] The 1984 AIF conference ventured to a new plateau with interchurch families' reflections on Christian initiation by a panel of children who had been baptized (and many of whom were already confirmed). The unique experiences of a generation of interchurch children and adolescents proffers new directions in pastoral care and theological appreciation of confirmation.

In French circles, the debate over confirmation (and for the Protestant churches, "profession of faith") led to the question: "Could one not seek an ecumenical form of confirmation which would leave the child his Christian identity, a child of God, with the possibility of living in the church which he would later choose?"[13] René Beaupère has sketched the history of the sacrament, giving evidence that details of the ritual were not "fixed," but open to adaptation to the renewal of Christian initiation. He suggested that interchurch couples, having several spiritual and ecclesial traditions, were among the "artisans" best equipped to contribute to an ecumenical reclaiming of confirmation.[14]

The vision of religious education sketched at the opening of Chapter 4 provides a special yardstick with which to measure successful confirmation catechesis. Is the preparation relatively quick and dominated by abstract doctrine? Or is the process of catechesis for mature faith a reflection on religious experience and ethical responsibility flowing from conversion and prayer? Is it individualistic or placed within the context of the community? A compelling example that promises a model for confirmation catechesis took place in Geneva in 1982. The striking identity of the interchurch candidates adds to their ecumenical sensitivity and creativity: they were handicapped persons. Ranging in age from seventeen to fifty years, these forty Roman Catholics and twelve Protestants, some physically and some mentally challenged persons, learned, worked, and engaged in recreation together each day. Most lived with their families. They could not understand why they should be separated for confirmation catechesis. The idea of a common celebration, presided over by the Roman Catholic bishop and a Reformed Church pastor, was born out of their questioning. Catechesis at six sites for sub-groups that accommodated particular configurations of candidates' special needs and ages was followed by a common retreat. Two successive eucharists were celebrated, each candidate receiving communion from his or her own pastor. Without ambiguity or confusion, these special candidates paved the way for an interchurch future. The retrospective remarks of the chaplains to the handicapped, who nurtured this event's process, deserve to be quoted:

At a later date, it is not impossible that our structures might adapt themselves, in turn, to this more intense common life. We do not know where we will be drawn on this road. We wish to remain open to the call of the Spirit. But we believe also that the Spirit speaks equally in our churches; the bond with our confessional families must be for us not a chain but an umbilical cord through which life passes. If we are more conscious of living in a somewhat special situation, we do not wish that it become marginal.[15]

Future Joint Catechesis

In 1977, Cardinal Johannes Willebrands, then president of the Vatican's Secretariat for Promoting Christian Unity, contributed an intervention at the international Synod of Bishops on catechesis and ecumenism. This steadfast Dutch veteran of ecumenical progress challenged the Roman Catholic Church to a "timely" and "urgent" undertaking: a study and implementation of joint catechesis. In keeping with a *koinonia* paradigm of restoring unity ("a communion of churches" concept, to which we turn in our next chapter), Willebrands sketched the possibility of common catechesis, "according to the degree of communion that exists." He introduced the question in the context of increasing numbers (admitting even the preponderance) of interchurch marriages.

Sometimes in the past catechesis actually was a source of prejudice, false interpretation, hatred for others. Today, in order to take care of the needs of the Church both local and universal, catechesis must form young people in truth and charity, avoiding polemics on the one hand and on the other hand avoiding "a false conciliatory approach which harms the purity of Catholic doctrine and obscures its assured genuine meaning" (Decree on Ecumenism, 11). However, this goal cannot be achieved unless there is instruction and understanding. All Christians are called to the work of promoting Christian unity because unity of Christians is the sign par excellence of the credibility and the truth of the Church. "At this point we wish to emphasize the sign of unity among all Christians as the way and instrument of evangelization" (*Evangelii Nuntiandi,* n. 77).[16]

Anne-Lise Nerfin, the Reformed Church pastor who served on the team preparing the handicapped for Geneva's 1982 confirmations, has focused lucidly the same issue: "The ecclesial community . . . is tied to catechesis like a tree to its branches. The community life dimension is not able to be forgotten for long." She encouraged endurance in the very local communities where ecumenical progress is curbed, where conditions and barriers are erected by "traditional" communities. The irritation, impatience, and weariness, she signaled, can convert these institutions.[17]

Summary

The sacraments of baptism, eucharist, and confirmation invite candidates and the gathered assembly of believers to a relationship with a God of love, revealed in Jesus Christ, and to a Christian ethical response in service to others' needs by acts of love and justice. Catechesis and liturgical celebrations of baptism, eucharist, and confirmation indeed empower us for the decisions of mature faith. They even help us discover a new paradigm for the restoration of unity among divided churches.

Future catechesis for interchurch and other children promises to reflect both the doctrinal consensus of reuniting churches, and ongoing experiences in the reconciliation process among individual Christians and their churches.

Notes

[1] *ARC Baptisms* (Los Angeles: EDEO-NADEO Joint Committee, 1983).

[2] *Interchurch Families* 2 (Winter 1979/80) 4. See also John Coventry, "United in Baptism," *The Tablet* 237 (1983) 555–57.

[3] *Foyers Mixtes* 24 (April 1974) 6–13.

[4] *Foyers Mixtes* 21 (October 1973) 16–17.

[5] *Foyers Mixtes* 65 (October–December 1984) 7–11.

[6] "Sacramental Theology and the World Church," *CTSA Proceedings* 39 (1984) 75. Later in this article, Wainwright refers to the "main text" of BEM which he calls "quite explicit about the transformative effect of baptism": "Those baptized are pardoned, cleansed and sanctified by Christ, and are given as part of their baptismal experience a new ethical orientation under the guidance of the Holy Spirit (n. 4)."

[7] *Interchurch Families* 5 (Summer 1981) C1ff.

[8] *Interchurch Families* 8 (Spring 1983) C4ff. This question is developed in detail with survey analysis by Ruth Reardon and Melanie Finch (eds.), *Sharing Communion: An Appeal to the Churches by Interchurch Families* (London: Collins, 1983), and Mary Bard, *Whom God Hath Joined* (London: Collins, 1987).

[9] *Foyers Mixtes* 66 (January–March 1985) 8f.

[10] See Gerard Austin, *The Rite of Confirmation: Anointing with the Spirit* (New York: Pueblo, 1985), and Aidan Kavanagh, *Confirmation: Origins and Reform* (New York: Pueblo, 1988).

[11] *Interchurch Families* 4 (Spring 1981) C1ff.

[12] Ibid. C4.

[13] *Foyers Mixtes* 33 (October–December 1976) 24–25.

[14] *Foyers Mixtes* 44 (July–September 1979) 26–28.

[15] *Foyers Mixtes* 57 (October–December 1982) 29–32.

[16] *Information Service* 36 (1978) 1–4.

[17] *Foyers Mixtes* 67 (April–June 1985) 11–14.

6. The Search for a Paradigm

Twenty-five years after the close of the Second Vatican Council, we are confronted with the complex task of appraising the resiliency of its vision of the church. How successfully have we implemented the vision of a renewed, intentionally ecumenical, servant church whose life, unity, and witness proclaims the "good news" of Jesus Christ to the world? This book has explored such questions from the perspective of a sleeping giant, awakening after a quarter century's stirrings—the emergence of interchurch families.

The English theologian John Coventry has described as a "time bomb" the council's setting in motion a revolutionary understanding of the church.[1] Once we admitted that other Christians were validly baptized, and once we called them "churches," it would only be a brief interlude before the implications of that admission caught up with the members of the body of Christ.

While I have grave misgivings about this violent metaphor of the "time bomb" to describe these principles, the analogy ventured by Coventry graphically impresses anyone serious about the future of ecumenism. Events in the lives of interchurch families outpace both our pastoral response and official church policies. Unless a concerted, honest recognition of the possibilities for more visible forms of unity in the lives of interchurch couples and their children develops, the alienation of these families from ecclesial life threatens to grow geometrically. The future of our churches depends more and more on the theological and pastoral integrity with which the interchurch family is welcomed and received. Can the churches afford any longer to be complacent when the body of Christ hemorrhages so painfully?

A surgeon plies skilled hands and microscopic new technology to catheterize clogged arteries and avoid the "time bomb" of a heart attack. Perhaps here Coventry's metaphor finds a more apt illustration. Are interchurch families serving as a diagnostic agent for the health of the body of Christ? Are they not recording for us alarms, signaling symptoms of unrecognized infirmity in the life of the church? Could we imagine interchurch family life, rooted in the gospel, witnessed in service and a commitment to human dignity, to global justice and peacemaking, as a muscular therapy to strengthen and to heal the body of the church? Could baptism and eucharist, even marriage itself, be revelatory in their experience, in ways that clarify and call the whole church to a deeper conversion?

Edward Schillebeeckx has constructed a foundational theology on the thesis that such surprising, negative experiences of contrast prove revelatory.

> [T]he constantly unforeseen content of new experiences keeps forcing us to think again. On the one hand, thought makes experience possible, while on the other, it is experience that makes new thinking necessary. Our thinking remains empty if it does not constantly refer back to living experience.[2]

By distinguishing between "experience" and "interpreta-tion," this Dutch theologian suggests an ongoing dialectical process: "the experience influences the interpretation and calls it forth, but at the same time the interpretation influ-ences the experience."[3]

How do interchurch families illustrate this dynamic process? Let me suggest that truly interchurch families, spouses and children who strive to live the unity of baptism and marriage, personify necessarily nagging questions for the divided churches. Their faith and experiences of Christ's grace in the "domestic church" of their household are vexed by institutional policies of churches that transpose denomi-national boundaries onto family life. In short, interchurch families have galvanized grassroots ecumenism and chal-lenged the official ecumenocrats to move beyond a tacit indifference which has postponed the restoration of Chris-tian unity. In effect, they pose the embarrassing question: Are the churches allergic to the possibilities for unity which the Holy Spirit offers us? Put more bluntly, interchurch fam-ilies question whether the churches can appeal to old alibis that have expired, and that no longer apply to the ecumeni-cal present and future.

For Schillebeeckx, a critical consideration of our inher-ited insights means seeing our interpretations in a different context which can correct, shatter, or give new direction. This book has evidenced that the marginal identity of inter-church families (in contrast to other families) provides such a revelatory insight into the nature of marriage and family life. For Schillebeeckx argues that "Truth comes near to us by the alienation and disorientation of what we have already achieved and planned," shattering our existing "normative-ness." Reality is disclosed, he concludes, in "the scandal, the stumbling block . . . [as] a surprising revelation." "In such experiences of what proves completely refractory to all our inventions, we shall finally also discover the basis for what we rightly call revelation."[4]

A Theory of Paradigm Shifts

It is no coincidence that Schillebeeckx refers to the pioneering work of Thomas S. Kuhn in his investigation of "the authority of new experiences."[5] Kuhn's *The Structure of Scientific Revolutions* introduced the notion of "paradigm shift" into scientific and other academic circles almost thirty years ago. One way of describing a paradigm is to speak of a dominant model, a conceptual or experiential explanation of reality. Kuhn had questioned how paradigms change in science. If paradigms are patterns, or sets of rules that define boundaries, then how do scientists exchange old paradigms for new sets of rules? How did we move from a flat earth mentality to a paradigm of the planet as a spherical globe? How did we move from an earth-centered concept of the physical universe to Galileo's heliocentric (sun-centered) universe? How, the theologian asks, do we shift from accepting historically separated churches to a communion (*koinonia*) of diverse but reunited churches?

What Kuhn's research has precipitated is an extraordinary self-examination for operative paradigms in various disciplines and institutions.[6] Because our paradigms exert powerful influence on the way in which we see the world, they also function as filters to screen information that is perceived. We have a difficult time accepting information that does not agree with our particular paradigm. Even scientists can distort information that disagrees with their paradigm, rather than acknowledge an exception to the rules. In this sense, paradigms operate as a source of prejudice. We select the information that best fits our paradigm and then try to ignore any conflicting information. What is obvious to a person with one paradigm is virtually imperceptible to a person with a new or different paradigm. One of Kuhn's persuasive examples from everyday experience presented a deck of playing cards. Some important alterations had been made on the face of a few of the cards. When a black ace of hearts appeared it was imperceptible to a quick glance; the same with a red seven of spades; and so forth. Our card deck paradigm had created expectations which inhibited our perceiving the information before our very eyes. Kuhn alerted us that our perceptions via paradigms dramatically influence our subsequent judgments and decisions by influencing (indeed distorting) those very perceptions.

Two effects of paradigms will relate directly to how interchurch families are received by the churches. First, the creators of new paradigms typically are found on the margins, outside the establishment. Therefore, because their vested interest in the old, failed paradigms has diminished, they are motivated to create new paradigms. And, second, the advocates of a new paradigm exhibit courage because it is not yet certain that the old, dominant model should be replaced by the new paradigm. Kuhn has emphasized:

> The person who embraces a new paradigm at an early stage must often do so in defiance of the evidence provided by the problem-solving. He must have faith that the new paradigm will succeed with the many large problems that confront it, knowing only that the older paradigm has failed in a few. A decision of that kind can only be made with faith.[7]

The reason such paradigm shifts are resisted involves the fact that more than a sequential or organic development is proposed by a new paradigm. The old paradigm is jeopardized because the new paradigm calls for "a fundamental reorganization of the science as a whole," meaning that we are not asked merely to "correct" our direction at mid-course, but to make a revolutionary mid-course change in our direction.[8]

Strategic Pastoral Planning

Interchurch couples quietly, almost unnoticed, have passed over where historic barriers and fortress ecclesiologies had once restricted and patronized them. The thesis of this book has simply affirmed that interchurch couples ought not to be perceived as a problem for the churches, but as a gift for the restoration of the unity of the church.

A Sunday front-page story in the December 11, 1988 *New York Times* reported that a Jewish-Christian couple's divorce litigation had developed into a quarrel over the custody and religious identity of their daughter.[9] The courts are now deciding questions of faith for children of couples from diverse religious traditions. This judicial development in the United States reveals only one implication (and a sad one, given the prevalence of divorce) of the dramatic increase in the frequency of marriage across denominational and religious boundaries. National statistics indicate that 40% of the Roman Catholic population are marrying non-Roman Catholic spouses.[10] Demographics in other denominations reveal an equally striking rise in the numbers of interchurch couples.[11] In an era when ecumenism has stalled at official levels of church unity, this grassroots phenomenon of religious intermarriage seems to augur a new hope of the "signs of the times" (*Gaudium et Spes,* 4). Is it a coincidental, ephemeral happening or a genuinely ecumenical event? An ecumenical paradigm shift?

In 1970 the Roman Catholic Church entered a new era in ecumenism with the publication of Pope Paul VI's *motu proprio, Matrimonia Mixta*.[12] The pastoral and theological currents of the Second Vatican Council converged in this papal directive, making possible the celebration of a sacramental marriage in the church of the bride or groom, with the priest or minister presiding at the liturgy of the respective church. In retrospect, this document reads as well-nigh reactionary: discouraging "mixed marriages," begrudgingly allowing the liturgy to take place in the other partner's church through the proviso of a "dispensation," or gingerly including the participation of the minister of the other church in the liturgy at the Catholic parish. But from the perspective of generations of veteran interchurch couples, the memories of humiliating "parlor" weddings in Catholic rectories, the unilateral demand that children be promised to the Catholic Church, and treatment of other Christians as baptized "unbelievers," Pope Paul VI's reforms have spared contemporary couples some of the wounds inflicted because of old divisions.

Karl Rahner wrote persuasively about the unity of the churches as an "actual possibility" in an important later work, where he noted, among others, mixed marriage couples "driven by impatience," practicing "on their own responsibility things that are officially and generally considered still to be impossible such as, for example, open communion." The context for his observation was the perception that the official church has stalled on the *status quo*. "Occasionally," he lamented, "one even gets the impression that the bar to ecumenical possibilities keeps being raised to higher and higher levels." He countered with the affirmation: "We hold that the ecumenical task has, and must have, one of the highest priorities for the responsibility and work of the Church."[13]

At the end of his career, this erudite Jesuit, once dubbed as "the quiet mover" behind the Second Vatican Council, reminded his readers, "I have always attempted to give a pastoral orientation to my theology." That very conviction lies behind this volume. By listening to the experiences of interchurch couples, the "joy and hope, the grief and anguish" (*Gaudium et Spes,* 1) of women and men faithfully living the unity of the "domestic church" (*Lumen Gentium,* 11) in their families, we can glimpse the horizon of our ecumenical future. As Rahner reflected on "the need to develop a strategic pastoral plan for the world church," he challenged us to consider the question of "the worldwide diaspora situation of the church." It is noteworthy that he included "mixed marriages" as a typical example of our diaspora experience—the church dispersed in a new secularized, post-Christian culture, without the structures and power of earlier eras. He observed, "This state of things . . . [has] not yet been given really systematic and courageous theological and pastoral reflection in the church."[14]

The familiar Rahnerian theme has centered the observations of these pages: "The church is the sacrament of the unplanned future, because the future is no other than the eternal incomprehensibility of God." Can one imagine Christians better equipped or more motivated to resuscitate such symbols of the coming church unity than interchurch couples and their children? Their role is presaged by Rahner's stimulating invitation, to which this book hopes to have offered a modest contribution.

> The church must and will look very different in its outward appearance from what we are accustomed to today. Is this future image to come upon the church unquestioned in advance? Is it something that "will happen" by small degrees without much foresight, or even be wrestled at times piecemeal from the contemporary situation? . . . Or must it not also, keeping in mind the

present-day state of collective human consciousness, be a task of the church, even if not a top priority, to *look ahead* and *plan ahead* as much as possible? Can and must there not be in the church a more farseeing world-wide strategy of pastoral care than hitherto? This seems to me a genuine question for the church, one that is not perceived clearly enough. Simply to pose this question, even though haltingly and gropingly, seems to me also a way in which pastoral theology can and must be pursued.[15]

Toward a New Paradigm

In the midst of a particularly lethargic panel presentation at the National Workshop on Christian Unity some years ago in Tulsa, the moderator concluded a panel's remarks with an invitation for comments or questions from the floor. The usual awkward silence of such moments visited the 1,500 participants at the event. Finally a woman walked to an aisle microphone. She commented that after listening to the panel for an hour and a half that morning she was perplexed at how they repeatedly used the metaphor "body of Christ" to describe the church. The woman happened to identify herself as a biologist. "Let me remind you of three simple facts about 'living organisms,'" she implored. "First, they respond to their environment. Second, they perform vital functions. And third, they reproduce themselves." For the first time in the two day meeting, spontaneous and thunderous applause erupted from the assembly. It was the sort of deafening, eye-opening *kairos* moment Roman Catholics have become accustomed to in the affirmation of catechumens at the Easter vigil, or candidates for the diaconate and priesthood at ordination.

Contemporary theologians have analyzed the implications of new models of the church which enhance this emphasis on the responding-living-reproducing church. As Avery Dulles remarked in his now classic *Models of the Church,* the only model which cannot be primary is the church as institution. In Dulles' schema, the church as a community of disciples lives the models of mystical community, sacrament, herald, and servant.[16] For the church in renewal, particular configurations of these models suggest the emphasis of distinctive Christian traditions. The most immediate associations are of "sacrament" with the Roman Catholic and Eastern Orthodox churches, and "herald" with reformation churches which historically placed greater emphasis on the centrality of proclamation of the word in the liturgy. But as we will examine in this chapter, the ecumenical movement has made available to each of the distinct traditions the treasures of the other. The ongoing renewal and simultaneous retrieval of models by the churches has led to a remarkable new convergence and surprising degrees of consensus.

The development of such an ecumenical theology of the church contradicts the inertia encountered by too many interchurch families in parishes and congregations. Thomas Rausch speaks of the use of the term "reception" in an ecumenical context to refer to "the acceptance by one church of a theological consensus arrived at with another church, and, ultimately, the recognition of the other church's faith and ecclesial life as authentically Christian." He appraises the lack of such reception as the emerging "crucial issue" for ecumenists because of "the discrepancy between the progress made in the ecumenical dialogues and the apparent inability of the sponsoring churches to build and move forward on the basis of what the dialogues have accomplished."[17]

The same symptoms are manifest in the lives of interchurch couples and their children, whose lived experience of unity in faith finds no pastoral "reception" or ecclesial manifestation of the implications of ecumenical progress. Cardinal Johannes Willebrands, former president of the Vatican's Council for Christian Unity, has carefully diagnosed the necessary transitional steps in the problem of "how theological consensuses and convergences can become ecclesial consensuses and convergences."[18] Interchurch families afford a "laboratory" of sorts in which the churches can discover the very principles and foundations of church unity fathomed by formal dialogues. Cardinal Willebrands' insistence on an ecclesial, not merely a juridical process is tested and refined in believers who struggle to respond to the gospel, perform community-building and servant ministries, and sacramentally hand on faith through the catechesis of their interchurch children.

The Second Vatican Council's Ecumenical Vision

A generation after the Second Vatican Council (1962–65), it helps to reconsider the Roman Catholic Church's declared principles of ecumenism vis-à-vis the experience of interchurch families. In a very direct sense, these principles set in motion the empowerment of interchurch families to serve as unique instruments for the restoration of the unity of the church. This is not to diminish the ecumenical responsibility of every member of the church, nor to shift the burden for ecumenical action. However, the nature of an interchurch family's commitment to church unity will be different, indeed perhaps more urgent because of family dynamics and the need to make visible the unity of faith they experience.

The Decree on Ecumenism

Pope John XXIII's appeal for the unity of all Christians auditioned as one of the major goals of the Second Vatican Council. If prospects for any serious ecumenical progress under the geriatric pope's leadership were discounted at the time, events have subsequently disabused the cynics. Those who expected preparatory commissions' retreading of the old treatises on the church to be rubber-stamped by the bishops assembled for the council found themselves in the middle of a revolution.[19] One such example was the inclusion of only a chapter on ecumenism in the initial drafts of the schema on the church. The council elected to return the text—one commentator described the process as a "frosty reception" by the council[20]—to the theological commission and demanded separate, entire texts on both ecumenism and the church's relationship to non-Christians.

A reading of the November 21, 1964 Decree on Ecumenism (*Unitatis Redintegratio*) orients Roman Catholics to a new context for understanding the ecumenical mission. Gone are the anathemas and condemnations of the past. In their place one finds the opening paragraphs of the decree acknowledging baptism as the source of our unity as Christians. Belief and baptism establish "some [certain], though imperfect communion" between Christians (n. 3). It is this same foundational unity of baptism that led the council to speak of other Christians as "churches and ecclesial communities" in the third chapter of the decree. "Baptism, therefore, constitutes the sacramental bond of unity existing among all who through it are reborn" (n. 22). At which point the council reminded the church that baptism is "only a beginning, a point of departure ... [ordained toward] a complete integration into eucharistic communion." In effect, the council admitted that it is abnormal for baptized Christians not to celebrate together the eucharist. This is the ultimate "scandal" of a divided church, "as if Christ himself were divided" (n. 1).

What captured the imagination of ecumenists was the clear goal identified by the decree: "all Christians will be gathered, in a common celebration of the eucharist" (n. 4). *How* that ultimate objective would be implemented remained an open question in the decree. *That* it is the defined objective of the Roman Catholic Church is unequivocally stated by the council. In effect, this meant that the council exhorted "*all* the Catholic faithful to recognize the signs of the times and to take an active and intelligent part in the work of ecumenism" (n. 4, emphasis added). In this text, interchurch families especially can be empowered to take initiatives. As the council put it, "In ecumenical work, Catholics must assuredly be concerned for their separated brethren . . . making the first approaches toward them" (n. 4).

Two Key Terms: "Separated Brethren" and "Subsists"

One approach to interpreting the import of the council's renewed understanding of the church in an ecumenical context is to examine particularly significant terms in the Decree on Ecumenism and the Constitution on the Church (*Lumen Gentium*). Because these terms are easily misunderstood, and because they carry technical meanings, their implications for interchurch families warrant a close reading and careful analysis. We will examine, in turn, two pivotal expressions: (1) "separated brethren"; (2) "subsists". Then in Chapter 7 we will consider the most compelling conciliar breakthrough affecting interchurch families, the understanding of a *koinonia,* or communion of churches, as the horizon of the ecumenical future.

"Separated Brethren"

The Roman Catholic entry into the ongoing ecumenical movement meant collaboration, not a unilateral initiative. Of all the phrases coined in the decree, that grating expression, "the separated brethren" (*fratres sejuncti*), most needs explanation—both as exclusive language (gender) and as ecumenically offensive. A cursory reading of the decree finds repeated use of the term, and repetition reinforces the misunderstanding of one-sided responsibility for the divided church. An effort to admit mutual blame and offer mutual forgiveness (n. 3; ch. 2, n. 7) pales beside the cumulative effect of "the separated brethren" refrain.

George Tavard has written a porous comment on this "separated brethren" rendering of the Latin text's *fratres sejuncti*. As one of the original drafters of the Decree on Ecumenism, he is eminently qualified to reconstruct the choice of the terminology. The subtlety of the Latin phrase has escaped our translations. For one, the phrase does not mean to place blame on a member which voluntarily divorces itself from the body. Our one-sided interpretations of the reformation have reinforced such parodies.[21]

Tavard has retrieved the authentic sense of the term, despite our clumsy translations. Its connotations suggest a summons to the churches to heal our tragic history of separation:

> First, the Latin term used to designate other Christians with whom Catholics ought to be in ecumenical dialogue was not *fratres separati,* but *fratres sejuncti.* This was done deliberately at the request of Cardinal Baggio, well known for his mastery of the Latin language: *separati,* he argued, would imply that there are and can be no relationships between the two sides; *sejuncti,* on the con-

trary, would assert that something has been cut between them, yet that separation is not complete and need not be definitive. The nuance does not come through easily in translation, but I would suggest "estranged brothers," rather than "separated." Thus the Secretariat and the Council worked on the basis that the result of the Reformation was partial lack of communion, not total separation.[22]

What the term *fratres sejuncti* implies is an anomaly, the existence of a situation that ought not to exist. Thus the divided church contradicts the ideal articulated by the council: all Christians gathered for a common celebration of the eucharist. To the extent that we fail to realize this goal, we are mutually exhorted to remedy this aberration. In this light, one can read this expression with a fuller sense of the Roman Catholic Church's call for all sisters and brothers baptized in the one Lord, Jesus Christ, to restore a unity which our churches have mutually broken. The separation is the result of all parties having refused to make visible the precious and fragile gift of baptismal incorporation into the body of Christ. None of us is spared the obligation of conversion and reform.

"Subsists"

Of all the terms found in Vatican Council II's documents, the word "subsists" as applied to the reality of Christ's Church in the Roman Catholic Church continues to occasion the most turbulent debate. Francis A. Sullivan has recently summed up the meaning of the council's change from "is" to "subsists in" to describe the connection between the church of Christ and the Roman Catholic Church by posing three questions: (1) What is the significance of this change from "is" to "subsists in" for our

thinking about the Catholic Church? (2) What is its significance for our thinking about other Christian communities?
(3) What is its significance for our thinking about the universal church of Christ? His conclusion deserves attention:
we cannot return to "the exclusive claim . . . that only the
[church] that is Roman Catholic has a right to be called
Church."[23]

In the spring and summer of 1963 this development was
set in motion when the preparatory commission of the council changed "is" to "subsists in" (*Unitatis Redintegratio* 4) to
reflect the significant admission that "many elements of
sanctification can be found outside [the Roman Catholic
Church's] total structure," and that these are "things properly belonging to the Church of Christ." Sullivan notes that
this implied that something of the "church" exists "beyond
the limits of the Catholic Church."[24] He argues persuasively
that the change to the term "subsists" marks the surrender of
"absolute and exclusive" identity between Christ's church
and the Roman Catholic Church. In other words, Roman
Catholics were now reoriented to a relationship with other
genuine churches—Eastern Orthodox, Anglican, and Protestant *churches* and not just individual Christians. Sullivan
points to the key to interpreting this admission in the Constitution on the Church; on the same day of its promulgation, November 21, 1964, Pope Paul VI explicitly pointed to
the "further explanations given in the Decree on Ecumenism," likewise promulgated that day.[25]

Our everyday usage of the word "subsist" further com-
plicates our comprehension of its meaning in the council's
documents. When we speak of someone living on a "subsistence" level, the unmistakable sense of "the *minimum* of food
and shelter to support life" paints a less than ideal situation.
However, it does suggest endurance, a persistent quality.
Sullivan points to the Constitution on the Church (*LG*, 8b)

which says that the Church of Christ subsisting in the Catholic Church "is not an ideal church" but the historical church tracing its continuity to the New Testament church entrusted to Peter and the other apostles. Nevertheless, as developed in the Decree on Ecumenism (*UR,* 2, 3e, 4c) the Roman Catholic Church enjoys a spiritual and visible unity intended by Christ, and it alone enjoys such a "subsistence level" of unity. Sullivan distinguishes this life of the Catholic Church with Christ's gifts of oneness, holiness, catholicity, and apostolicity from "a state of eschatological perfection." He captures this subtle distinction:

> There is no question of denying that a non-Catholic community, perhaps lacking much in the order of sacrament, can achieve the *res* [reality], the communion of the life of Christ in faith, hope, and love, more perfectly than many a Catholic community. The means of grace have to be well to achieve their full effect, and the possession of a fullness of means is no guarantee of how well they will be used.[26]

A reactionary narrowing of this recognition of other churches is evidenced in the Vatican Congregation for the Doctrine of the Faith's criticism of Leonardo Boff's book, *Church, Charism and Power.* Sullivan disputes the CDF's justification of the claim that "there exists only one subsistence of the true Church"[27] because it contradicts the explanations we have just examined in the Decree on Ecumenism. He points to the Constitution on the Church itself (*LG,* 15). What is at stake is an attempt to reduce the other churches to something less than churches, having only "*elements* of the church."[28] The document, however, speaks here of other Christians "who indeed recognize and receive other sacraments in their own churches or ecclesiastical communities." In concert with the Decree on Ecumenism (*UR*, 3), which speaks of the salvific role of the "liturgical actions" of these churches *as churches,* having been "by no means deprived of significance and importance in the mystery of salvation,"[29] the council had wound tightly the mainspring which would begin ticking off John Coventry's "time bomb" of future implications.

From another vantage, Cardinal Johannes Willebrands, an original 1960 staff member of the Vatican's Secretariat for Promoting Christian Unity and later President of the Vatican's Council for Christian Unity, offered a similar interpretation of these two texts (*LG*, 8 and *UR*, 4). The occasion was two major speeches in the United States, May 5 and 8, 1987. He has called attention to the dropping of the adjective "Roman" in the first document. This accommodated the recognition of the status of the Eastern Orthodox churches as truly Catholic churches, though not in full communion with the bishop of Rome. "While the Council did not hesitate to speak of the separated Eastern Churches as 'particular churches' without qualification, it was the mind of the [Conciliar Theological] Commission that the western communities that lack the full reality of the Eucharist—without attempting to decide which ones these were—still have a truly ecclesial character, and are at least analogous to particular churches of the one Church of Christ." But he ventured further in reconstructing the shift in terms. Willebrands has placed the much discussed text (*LG*, 15) in the perspective of the mystery of grace, suggesting that the change "has a bearing far beyond the strictly institutional."

It has to do with grasping the implications of belonging to Christ. The standpoint is not juridical but Christological. The problem of *subsistit in* cannot be properly understood from any other standpoint.

In this sense, Willebrands insists, our use of *church* ought not be restrictive or exclusive because the Roman Catholic Church "does not exhaust that [mystical] body."[30] The division of the church "has not cut deep," he argues, "it has not touched unity in Christ, the unity of charity and peace, that alliance of perfect unity which has banished darkness and bathed us in new light."[31] Like Sullivan, Willebrands interprets the Constitution on the Church (*LG*, 8, 15) in light of the Decree on Ecumenism (*UR*, 3, 4).

While other churches lack the "fullness" claimed for the Catholic Church, Willebrands notes, belonging to the Church of Christ is "Christocentric" and, therefore, grace comes to the baptized in other churches. "There are no vagrant baptized," he emphasizes. Their belonging to the church takes place "in the community, Lutheran, Methodist, or Baptist, etc."[32] He concludes by rebutting suggestions that the council documents harbor contradictory ecclesiologies, and then makes an extraordinary connection.

> *Subsistit in* cannot be authentically understood except in the setting of ecclesiology of communion, and then only if communion is seen not simply horizontally nor merely as between Christians or Christian communities, but also and in the first place as communion with God himself. The statement of the first Johannine epistle is here of capital importance, whatever the circumstances which explain it: "Fellowship is with the Father and with his Son Jesus Christ" (1 Jn 1:3).[33]

A third term, *koinonia,* or that "communion" of baptized Christians with God, Christ, one another, and the estranged churches, builds upon the progress of our deeper appreciation of "estranged brothers" and "subsists." Here we will discover a new paradigm for imagining the restored unity of diverse churches.

Summary

This chapter has considered how interchurch families concretely represent an instance of Edward Schillebeeckx's negative experiences of contrast as a revelatory moment for the church. From the margins of parish and congregational culture, they constantly remind us that marriage and family relationships ground many of the lived experiences of grace. The phenomenon of interchurch families affords a new paradigm in the sense that the rules and boundaries which segregated the divided churches can no longer be persuasively applied when evaluating their unique needs or gifts. As the churches develop future strategic planning, interchurch families provide a new paradigm of actual possibilities for ecclesial unity. When we revere them as integral to the living body of Christ, then we can reexamine the Second Vatican Council's principles of ecumenism in a more nuanced and constructive sense. To speak knowledgeably in terms of "separated brethren," or the church as it "subsists" in the Roman Catholic Church, does not discredit other Christians or churches, but summons us to a deeper *koinonia,* a communion of churches, for which interchurch families provide a living paradigm.

Notes

[1]"Theological Reflections," in Mary Bard, *Whom God Hath Joined* (London: Collins, 1987) 111–17.

[2]Edward Schillebeeckx, *Christ: The Experience of Jesus as Lord* (New York: Seabury, 1980) 32.

[3]Ibid. 35.

[4]Ibid. For an analogous sense of the contrasting experience as revelatory, see the work of Jean Vanier, whose l'Arche communities for the physically and mentally challenged demonstrate their greater knowledge about our humanness in the ways of the

human heart. The hands and heads of these "handicapped" persons ordinarily do not work as quickly or with the dexterity of ours; but they have what makes them quintessentially human—hearts that spontaneously (and without masked subtleties) love and seek to be loved. For an excellent analysis of the l'Arche spirituality see Michael Downey, *A Blessed Weakness: The Spirit of Jean Vanier and L'Arche* (San Francisco: Harper and Row, 1986).

[5]Schillebeeckx, 31. The entire first chapter, "The Authority of New Experiences" (pp. 30–64), integrates the scientific discussion of paradigm changes with Schillebeeckx's analysis of experience in a theological anthropology.

[6]For a good popular presentation and applied study of Kuhn's paradigm shift theory, see Joel Barker, *Discovering the Future: The Business of Paradigms* (Lake Elmo: ILI Press, 1985).

[7]Thomas S. Kuhn, *The Structure of Scientific Revolutions* (Chicago: University of Chicago, 1962) 157.

[8]Hans Küng, "Paradigm Change in Theology: A Proposal for Discussion," *Paradigm Change in Theology: A Symposium for the Future,* ed. Hans Küng and David Tracy (New York: Crossroad, 1989) 20–21.

[9]*The New York Times* (December 11, 1988) 1.

[10]Dean R. Hoge and Kathleen M. Ferry, *Empirical Research on Interfaith Marriage in America* (Washington, DC: USCC, 1981).

[11]W.C. Roof and William McKinney, *American Mainline Religion: Its Changing Shape and Future* (New Brunswick: Rutgers University Press, 1987) 58–70, 155–57, 203.

[12]*Acta Apostolicae Sedis* 62 (1970) 257–59.

[13]Karl Rahner and Heinrich Fries, *The Unity of the Churches: An Actual Possibility* (Philadelphia/New York: Fortress Press and Paulist Press, 1985) 2–3, 5.

[14]Karl Rahner, "Epilogue: Perspectives on Pastoral Ministry in the Future," in Walbert Bühlmann, *The Church of the Future: A Model for the Year 2001* (Maryknoll: Orbis, 1986) 185, 191, 194–96.

[15] Ibid. 197.

[16]Avery Dulles, *Models of the Church* (Garden City: Doubleday, 1974).

[17]T. Rausch, *Authority and Leadership in the Church* (Wilmington: Michael Glazier, 1989) 103; further bibliography on formal "reception" and its importance in ecumenical theology can be found in numerous commentaries on the 1982 Faith and Order Commission of the World Council of Church's *Baptism, Eucharist and Ministry* text.

[18]Johannes Willebrands, "The Ecumenical Dialogue and Its Reception," *Bulletin/Centro pro unione* 27 (1985) 6, as quoted in Rausch, *Authority,* 104.

[19]See Alberic Stackpoole (ed.), *Vatican II: By Those Who Were There* (Minneapolis: Winston, 1986).

[20]Francis A. Sullivan, "The Significance of the Vatican II Declaration That the Church of Christ 'Subsists in' the Roman Catholic Church," in René Latourelle (ed.), *Vatican II: Assessment and Perspectives* (New York: Paulist Press, 1989) II, 273.

[21]One recent reminder of this misreading of the roots of the reformation came in the four hundred and fiftieth anniversary celebrations of the Augsburg Confession (1530) in the excellent study of Joseph Burgess (ed.), *The Role of the Augsburg Confession: Catholic and Lutheran Views* (Philadelphia/New York: Fortress Press and Paulist Press, 1980).

[22]George H. Tavard, "Reassessing the Reformation," *One in Christ* 19 (1983) 360–61.

[23]Sullivan, II: 275, 284–85.

[24]Ibid. 274.

[25]Ibid. 274–75.

[26]Ibid. 278–79.

[27]Ibid. 280–83.

[28]Sullivan adds: "The word 'subsistere' by itself does not necessarily connote such structural integrity as is claimed for the Catholic Church. In fact, the Council used the same word, with the qualifier 'ex parte,' 'partially,' or 'incompletely,' when it said that certain Catholic traditions and institutions 'subsist' in the Anglican Communion (*UR* 13b). This has to be kept in mind if the question is raised whether the Church of Christ can be said to 'subsist' also in other Christian churches" (279).

[29]Ibid. 282–83.

[30]Johannes Willebrands, "Vatican II's Ecclesiology of Communion," *One in Christ* 23 (1987) 183.

[31]Ibid. 184.

[32]Ibid. 189.

[33]Ibid. 190.

7. A Communion of Churches
—*Koinonia*

Once the Roman Catholic Church had recognized the gathered assemblies of other baptized Christians as "churches and ecclesial communities," part of the *one* church of Christ, the ancient question of how distinct churches would relate to one another uncoiled. As so often in the past, ecumenists turned to a biblical concept from the New Testament, the Greek word *koinonia,* to capture the genius of unity in diversity.

Scholars point to the authoritative collection of New Testament books, the *canon* of books that "measure up" to the norm of faith, as one of the early church's experiences of unity in diversity. It surprises many Christians to learn that such consensus on the scripture canon did not come before the fourth century when Athanasius, bishop of Alexandria, first definitively enumerated the canon's twenty-seven books. And it resulted largely because earlier attempts to define a canon were judged inadequate. For example, in the second century the church rejected as a canon Marcion's anti-Jewish collection of Pauline letters and Luke's gospel. The process of achieving agreement from churches and leaders in an expansive Christianity set a precedent for decision-making and authority. What resulted was a New

Testament that holds in tension some widely divergent understandings of the church, Christ, faith, and discipleship. But on the essentials they are in agreement. In fact, this model of diversity within the New Testament continues to serve as a corrective to extremes.

When the Second Vatican Council appealed to the restoration of "full communion" (*UR,* 3) for the churches, this balanced *koinonia* model of unity in diversity was retrieved. To appreciate its nuances, it is helpful to consider other historical and familiar models of church unity which modern ecumenists have suggested.

The earliest efforts of ecumenists in the twentieth century resulted in irenic, constructive agreements, often labeled as a comparative ecclesiology. But these thoughtful statements often overlooked the underlying diversity of methods and style that various churches and traditions presuppose. Plateaus in the history of ecumenical dialogue are easily traced in the Faith and Order Commission of the World Council of Churches. For example, at its 1952 meeting in Lund, Sweden there was a dramatic shift to a "christocentric" method. By seeing Christ as the common center of their identity as church, the churches, it was suggested, could then better relate to one another. The pursuit of truth (and its formulation by ecumenists) takes on a decidedly different trajectory from this christocentric vantage. In 1961 at New Delhi, the Faith and Order Commission agreed that "unity does not imply simple uniformity of organization, rite or expression." Diversity was emerging with voice and strength. This same session tethered particularity and universality in the quest for "organic unity." They spoke of unity conceived as "the fully committed fellowship" of "all God's people in each place" and yet "united with the whole Christian fellowship in all places and all ages." By 1975 at their Nairobi, Kenya meeting this vision of unity in common sacraments, common prayer, joint witness and service expanded into a "conciliar fellowship of local churches which are themselves truly united."

Lukas Vischer, former director of the Faith and Order Commission, offers one conceptualization of models of church unity. It ranges from: (1) John Wesley's "spiritual harmony"; (2) the Augsburg Confession's "the gospel rightly preached and the sacraments rightly administered"; (3) episcopal structure; (4) tradition; (5) a common willingness to act together.[1]

Thomas Rausch offers perhaps the clearest spectrum of models of church unity. He categorizes four models: (1) organic union; (2) conciliar fellowship; (3) reconciled diversity; (4) communion of churches. The imprint of the Faith and Order Commission's deliberations is evident in these terms. What Rausch offers with these models is a critique of strengths and weaknesses. The organic union model affords visible institutional continuity, but can fall into the "least common denominator" mode. Conciliar fellowship would overcome overlapping jurisdictions of competing churches, but forfeits both confessional identity and the desired worldwide ("catholic") character and universal teaching authority. Reconciled diversity preserves the range of confessional identities and church structures while providing a deliberative organ, but does not build on sufficient doctrinal consensus or adequate structures for mission and church life. The communion model preserves the autonomy and diversity of churches, with the suggestion by Rausch that the relationship of Roman Catholic religious orders and congregations (with distinct charism, spirituality, and mission) to the church could be analogous for Protestant churches. This leaves open the question of how these "particular churches" would relate to the circles of authority at regional and universal levels.[2]

Any effort to reconstruct the models of church unity invariably progresses to the *koinonia* or communion model. Its emergence from both Faith and Order's texts and the Second Vatican Council's documents is no mere coincidence. When the definitive history of this chapter of ecumenism is written, the shuttle diplomacy carried on by the same theologians contributing to both series of events will illustrate how unity in theological diversity has precipitated this ecumenical convergence.

One of the earliest and most significant auditions for the *koinonia* model was the 1970 speech by Cardinal Willebrands in which he described the "communion of communions" as a "plurality of types (*typoi*) with the communion of the one, universal church.

> Where there is a long coherent tradition, commanding men's love and loyalty, creating and sustaining a harmonious and organic whole of complementary elements, each of which supports and strengthens the others, you have the reality of a *typos.* Such complementary elements are many. A characteristic theological method and approach (historical perhaps in emphasis, concrete and mistrustful of abstraction) is one of them. . . . A characteristic liturgical expression is another. It has its own psychology; here a people's distinctive experience of the one divine Mystery will be manifest.[3]

Among these "types" of church are the Lutheran type, the Presbyterian type, the Orthodox type, the Roman Catholic type, the Disciples type, and so forth. The Second Vatican Council not only retrieved this very *koinonia* model in the ecumenical sphere, animating its vision of restoring "full communion" with our sister churches. But Roman Catholicism rediscovered the plurality within its own communion as a global reality. This was the major theme of the Pastoral Constitution on the Church in the Modern World (*Gaudium et Spes*), exploring how the Roman Catholic Church could renew its mission in a diversity of cultural and social realities. Karl Rahner dubbed this the great event of the council, the bishops' affirmation of a "world church" that no longer imposed exclusively European forms or modes of expression on third world and other Christian communities. The same apostolic faith could be "inculturated" in a Roman Catholic communion blessed with a rich diversity of spiritualities, liturgies, and even theologies.[4]

Within the Decree on Ecumenism (*UR*, 16–18), the council addressed the *koinonia* with the Orthodox churches, the "churches of the east," expressly valuing the "diversity of customs and observances [which] only adds to her beauty and contributes greatly to carrying out her mission." And here the council even broached the issue of "legitimate variety . . . in theological expressions of doctrine." Earlier in the decree (*UR*, 11) the term " 'hierarchy' of truths" had been introduced as a breakthrough for "comparing doctrines." Indeed, this text meant that "the way will be opened" for a unity in essentials, while " 'imposing no burden beyond what is indispensable' (Acts 15:28)" (*UR*, 18).

When the council turned to the "separated churches and ecclesial communities in the west," the *koinonia* model radiated a new context for unity. The decree is frank in speaking of "weighty differences" (*UR*, 19) of social, psychological, and cultural character, and especially of a theological nature. However, it proceeds to speak of the "communion" in Christ as the source and center (*UR*, 20); baptism is "the sacramental bond of unity" "ordained . . . toward a complete integration into eucharistic communion" (*UR*, 22); and even while questioning the ordination of reformation church ministers, dialogue on eucharist becomes paramount because their celebrations "profess that it signifies life in communion with Christ" (*UR,* 22).[5]

A Case Study in *Koinonia:* ARCIC [6]

As we saw in Chapter 6, theologians and scientists in other fields who converse about various models identify particular models which become so dominant and stable as ways of understanding reality that they are named "paradigms." One of the virtues of a new paradigm is that it allows us to experience and understand realities we did not perceive in the former paradigms. That, in turn, affects our judgments and decisions, making possible what was once unthinkable. For interchurch couples and families, the *koinonia* paradigm has challenged the churches to reexamine the nature and mission of the church. We will focus on a particular bilateral dialogue which has profited immensely from such a use of *koinonia.*

In March 1966, the historic meeting between Pope Paul VI and Archbishop Michael Ramsey of Canterbury led to a decision to begin a formal dialogue between the Roman Catholic Church and the churches of the Anglican Communion. In introducing *The Final Report* (1981) of the first Anglican-Roman Catholic International Commission (ARCIC), *koinonia* was credited by the authors as "fundamental" to all its statements. Indeed, it looms as the architectonic, or structural, principle.

> The Son of God has taken to himself our human nature, and he has sent upon us his Spirit who makes us so truly members of the body of Christ that we too are able to call God "Abba, Father" (Rom. 8:15; Gal. 4:6). Moreover, sharing in the same Holy Spirit, whereby we become members of the same body of Christ and adopted chil-

dren of the same Father, we are also bound to one another in a completely new relationship. *Koinonia* with one another is entailed by our *koinonia* with God in Christ. This is the mystery of the Church.[7]

Such conversion to Christ results in empowerment by the Holy Spirit (*FR,* 1). But it is when ARCIC turns to two pivotal issues, authority and eucharist, that the implications of this *koinonia* become rejuvenating for the dialogue.

First, ARCIC relieved some of the tension from polarizing the primacy of the bishop of Rome against the conciliar sharing of authority. ARCIC relocated a "balance" and even ventured to speak of the *koinonia* realized among local churches in a dialectical relationship with the communion of churches at a universal level. In a striking advance, the text envisioned "that communion with the bishop of Rome does not imply that submission to an authority which would stifle the distinctive features of the local churches" (*FR,* "Authority in the Church I," [1976] 12). The mediating figure of the local bishop in both Roman Catholic and Anglican life personifies the unity *within* the local church (given all its uniqueness) and its unity *with* the larger "communion of communions" or universal church.[8]

The second issue, eucharist, fathomed an even more valuable insight. It provides a classic example of a changed method (or use of a new paradigm) for pursuing ecumenical dialogue. The question is no longer one of reconciling irreconcilable expressions of apostolic faith. The question is to move beyond these limited, historical formulations and give voice to new, more adequate expressions of the common apostolic faith. Thus, ARCIC was able to achieve a "substantial consensus" on the understanding of eucharist because it refused to be lured into reenacting quarrels that decoyed the churches from essential truths. ARCIC's conclusions about "The Presence of Christ in the Eucharist" transcend the medieval understanding of "transubstantiation" without denying its affirmation of the "*fact*" of Christ's presence.

> The ultimate change intended by God is the transformation of human beings into the likeness of Christ. The bread and wine *become* the sacramental body and blood of Christ in order that the Christian community may *become* more truly what it already is, the body of Christ (*FR,* "Elucidation: Eucharistic Doctrine" [1979]).

Our progress toward *koinonia,* or full communion, as an institutional agreement is not the final goal. Much as that unity lived in a eucharistic communion (which interchurch families and ecumenists long to enjoy) summons us as an object of concern, it is only a step in the ever-longer pilgrimage. Ultimately, the eucharistic communion of Anglicans and Roman Catholics, or any future configuration of formal intercommunion among churches, will take us beyond self-consciousness that we might serve others. *Koinonia* is for the purpose of service, the *diakonia* which the New Testament and apostolic tradition identifies as the essence of Christian life. It is this understanding of the eucharist which the Faith and Order Commission of the World Council of Churches proposed in its remarkable consensus statement of 1982, *Baptism, Eucharist and Ministry.* It is the insight which ARCIC's *koinonia* interpretation of eucharist has made manifest: *becoming* the body of Christ for the transformation of the world.

> The eucharist embraces all aspects of life. It is a representative act of thanksgiving and offering on behalf of the whole world. The eucharistic celebration demands reconciliation and sharing among all those regarded as

brothers and sisters in the one family of God and is a
constant challenge in the search for appropriate relationships in social, economic and political life. . . . All
kinds of injustice, racism, separation and lack of freedom are radically challenged when we share in the body
and blood of Christ. Through the eucharist the all-
renewing grace of God penetrates and restores human
personality and dignity. The eucharist involves the
believer in the central event of the world's history. As
participants in the eucharist, therefore, we prove incon-
sistent if we are not actively participating in this ongoing
restoration of the world's situation and the human
condition.[9]

Did not Jesus ask, after washing the disciples' feet at the
meal, "Do you know what I have done to you?" His com-
mand, recalled in our churches each Holy Thursday as we
begin the ancient triduum liturgies, makes unmistakable the
link between eucharist and the servant-church: "You also
ought to wash one another's feet" (Jn 13:12–14).

Ramifications for Interchurch Families

The ramifications of the *koinonia,* or communion of
churches, paradigm prove to be liberating for interchurch
families and pastoral ministers. We first glimpsed this revi-
sionist starting point in René Beaupère's forceful audition
of the concept of double belonging (Chapter 1). He asked
whether a more nuanced understanding of the Second
Vatican Council's teaching of a certain, though imperfect
communion (*UR,* 3) between the churches does not obligate
us to a more positive approach. In other words, given the
certain (though imperfect) union we already enjoy by virtue
of a common baptism, what interim steps toward full communion now must follow? And who better than the inter-

church families to lead the way? We cannot void the council's declared commitment to the restoration of full eucharistic communion with all the baptized (*UR,* 4). When the churches celebrate the marriage of interchurch spouses, we make visible such a progressive step by naming this union a sacrament.

With the arrival of children in an interchurch family, the next progressive steps toward fuller visible unity become strikingly incarnate for the churches. These families occasion the churches' coming to grips with a foundational baptismal unity in a dramatic liturgical event. For when the child's baptism is celebrated by the church, in the unique, concrete reality of interchurch families, the churches set in motion a trajectory that points irreversibly to the goal of full communion in the eucharist. In Chapters 3, 4, and 5 we traced the progressive steps leading from joint religious education and catechesis to genuine possibilities for joint confirmation experiences, and eucharistic sharing within interchurch families. Subtle and positive provisions of canon law attest to the undeniable rights of interchurch families (among others) to avail themselves of possibilities for visible unity that already exist within the churches' mutual commitment to restore the unity of the one church of Christ.

The conclusion of Chapter 6's search for a new paradigm recalled Karl Rahner's stern reminder that our ecumenical imperatives leave us open to "the church of the unplanned future." And so we come full circle, to the opening scenario of the first chapter, and our caravan of interchurch families at the crossroad: existing signposts failed to admit their presence, and callously attempted to separate interchurch family members from one another. Interchurch families help us plan the future church when their experience informs and converts the engineers who design the signposts. These families have explored the frontiers of full communion, and their eyes, minds, and hearts already live the council's vision of the ecumenical future. Where better to receive news of the pilgrim's progress toward full communion than in the lives of interchurch families who have walked what others only talk?

In the final analysis, interchurch families offer the ultimate reminder that the *koinonia* we seek as churches will always be unfinished because it exacts an ongoing conversion that will not be exhausted by institutional agreement. The French speak of *la vie provisoire,* a provisional lifestyle that adapts to unexpected demands, immediate needs that cannot be neglected while we exercise on philosophical abstractions. Family life is saturated with these moments of interdependence, unselfish response, and unexpected enrichment in attending to one another. It affords a microcosm of community. Family *koinonia* inevitably leads to *diakonia,* which strengthens and renews *koinonia.* And this native capacity for unity and service enlarges by celebrating these family experiences in the wider life of the church and its mission.

Summary

We have moved in this chapter through a series of reflections on *koinonia* (communion) and finally to *diakonia* (service). Here unfolds the whole new context in which interchurch families have been empowered to claim their unique personification of the church. Their intimacy, ecstasy, and fecundity[10] as wife and husband, and children, are recognized as a presence of Christ in their lives. Within the horizon of our new context for understanding the developing ecumenical movement (the *koinonia* or communion of churches), the future church is dawning through these pioneering interchurch families' proffer of unimagined gifts.

Notes

[1]Lukas Vischer, "Drawn and Held Together by the Reconciling Power of Christ," *Ecumenical Review* 26 (1974) 172–73, as detailed in Michael Kinnamon, *Truth and Community: Diversity and Its Limits in the Ecumenical Movement* (Grand Rapids: Eerdmans, 1988) 75–77.

[2]Thomas P. Rausch, *Authority and Leadership in the Church: Past Directions and Future Possibilities* (Wilmington: Michael Glazier, 1989) 120–32. The terminology for evolving models of church unity proves to be a highly nuanced maze. For example, in Anglican circles the term "organic union" and "organic unity" do not hold the negative connotations Rausch and others associate with it. See, for example, *The Emmaus Report: A Report of the Anglican Ecumenical Consultation 1987* (London: Church House Publishing, 1987), especially Chapters 1 and 2: "Christian Unity: The Gift, the Vision and the Way," and "Churches in Full Communion." Quoting from the ACC's 1981 study, *Full Communion*: "Organic union has consistently been a term used in Lambeth Conferences and in the Anglican Consultative Council to describe the goal of Christian unity. 'We believe that the Organic Union of all Christians and all Churches in each place, and of each place with every other, is the will of Christ'" (30). The report proceeds to recall that the 1952 Lund meeting of the Faith and Order Commission advocated the term "full communion" to describe relations within the same denominational or confessional family, and "intercommunion" to describe varying degrees of relation between churches of one communion with a church or churches of another.

[3]"Moving Toward a Typology of Churches," *Catholic Mind* 68 (1970) 35–42.

[4]Karl Rahner, "A Basic Theological Interpretation of the Second Vatican Council," *Theological Investigations* 20 (New York: Crossroad, 1981) 77–89.

[5]Cf. Francis Sullivan's cogent note: "It is surely significant that in UR 22c, the Council does not use the term 'Churches and ecclesial communities,' but only 'ecclesial communities,' as the subject of the sentence in which it denies the presence of the

'genuine and total reality of the Eucharistic mystery' because of the 'lack of the sacrament of Orders.' That this was the mind of the Commission in making this distinction is also clearly indicated in its *Relatio,* AS, 111/2, 335, where it recognized the propriety of speaking of the Orthodox and Old Catholic 'Churches,' precisely because they had preserved valid orders and the full reality of the Eucharist" (286 n.24).

[6]See my development of a more detailed study of ARCIC for EDEO-NADEO's 1984–88 series of reports, collected in *ARC Soundings* (Latham: University Press of America, 1990).

[7]Anglican-Roman Catholic International Commission, *The Final Report* (Cincinnati: Forward Movement Publications, 1982) n. 5. All quotations of ARCIC I are taken from this edition.

[8]Cf. J. Robert Wright (ed.), *A Communion of Communions: One Eucharistic Fellowship* (New York: Seabury, 1979).

[9]"Eucharist," *Baptism, Eucharist and Ministry* (Geneva: World Council of Churches, 1982) n. 20.

[10]See Michael Downey, *Clothed in Christ: The Sacraments and Christian Living* (New York: Crossroad, 1987) 147–53.

8. Reflections on Future Directions

Each Pentecost Sunday, the covenant between two large, suburban Episcopal and Roman Catholic parishes in Louisville occasions a picnic celebration. Hundreds of people gather for potluck dinner under shade trees, passing the late spring afternoon in games, conversation, and laughter. It is the epitome of grassroots ecumenism, cultivated now over twenty years through a broad spectrum of joint activities. The climax of the afternoon comes with a tug-of-war game in which members of the two churches stretch across the parking lot and compete, lined up behind respective pastors. Long-time participants recollect that oddsmakers have occasionally given the edge to the parish whose pastor carries a decided weight advantage. One interchurch mother narrates her experience on such a Pentecost, when her six year old son Tommy came racing up to her as the rope tautened. "Mommy, mommy," he pleaded, "which side am I on?" His ordeal personifies the subtle, unconscious ways in which even the most conscientious of parishes can marginalize and exclude interchurch families. This mother's heartache at that moment reveals how unwittingly we create division and separation, even in moments of good-humored games. The event, however, has seared itself into the psyche of these two parishes, prompting them to recognize the presence of interchurch children and spouses, and to consider the ordeals which we unknowingly, yet unjustly, create for them.

The faces of interchurch families have all too easily been "air brushed" from the collective portrait of our parishes and congregations. This book has attempted to appreciate the gift of interchurch families, to refocus on their experience, and to appropriate from their faith and lives new energy and hope for the churches' reunion. These pages have analyzed what the first chapter described as the phenomenon of interchurch spouses, both of whom remain active in their respective churches and take a conscientious role in the religious education of children. Their experience contradicts previous generations' dire warnings about the prospects for "mixed marriages" surviving. What I have invited all our churches to consider is how questions about interchurch families were posed in the wrong way in so much past pastoral practice. There is a new paradigm (retrieved from the New Testament) for the unity of the churches, the *koinonia,* or communion of distinct churches. Already interchurch couples live intimately the reality of this model of Christian unity explored in Chapter 6.

The joint international commission named by the Roman Catholic Church and the World Methodist Council evidences the developing new context in which interchurch marriages should be assessed. In its 1971 Denver Report, the dialogue team began addressing the "conflict and difficulties" inherent in these marriages. To their credit, they did also remark: "But the conflict and agony in such marriages has not been created by positive law and will not be resolved by positive law." A decade later, the 1981 Honolulu Report of the joint commission backed away from identifying interchurch families as the "problem":

This same realistic assessment of the widespread disregard of the meaning of marriage must be brought to bear on any consideration of interchurch marriages. These are often spoken of as posing a "problem" in terms of doctrine, ecclesiastical polity and pastoral care. They are in fact a problem to those marrying only if they belong to the small minority within a minority, that is those who are not only Church members but also take the responsibilities of membership seriously. Consequently those who do belong to different Churches and who seek guidance concerning interchurch marriage should be welcomed for their faithful concern and not chided for posing a problem, especially since they can hardly be held responsible for the division between our Churches which is the underlying cause of the problem. Again, this is not to advocate a disregarding of the difficulties nor a weakening of discipline concerning marriage. It is to urge that what we already hold in common should be used as a basis for marriage and family life that reflects the will of God in Christ for human society.[1]

Michael Kinnamon recently articulated with new energy the goal of the ecumenical movement. It bears special importance for interchurch families because he has reminded us that the purpose of dialogue and collaboration is not "to think and act alike," but "to expand the range of unlikeness that we can legitimately embrace as our own—because Christ has made it his own."[2] This attitude and understanding of the ecumenical movement proves a bellwether for future directions in ecumenism, and particularly for the role of interchurch families. In a commentary on his own writing on ecumenical "unity in diversity," Kinnamon asks the ultimate question: "Isn't time running out on our idolatrous divisions?"[3]

William McConville has coined a new term, "*ecclesia-*

dicy," to describe *"those who suffer because of the church* rather than those who suffer, often heroically, on behalf of the church."[4] This play on the term "theodicy" (to justify the ways of God, i.e. the existence of evil and suffering vis-à-vis our human condition) distinguishes *sin* from *tragedy*. We can all identify sins of particular clergy, hierarchy, or other baptized believers, as well as more recent sins embedded in structures of our society (industrial pollution, economic systems), and the distinct victims of such sins. But there is another reality, the tragic, which McConville has borrowed from Richard Sewall's *The Vision of Tragedy*. One characteristic applies especially to the experience of interchurch families.

> The tragic illumines human suffering. Confronted by a disorder which they did not choose, human beings respond with action which "involves the ultimate risk, and pushes [them] to the very limits. . . ." They find themselves in "boundary-situations" which demand decisions. In freedom a choice is made and this choice leads to suffering. The choice, however, is never unambiguously clear; it involves a murky mixture of good and evil. The suffering thus engendered is fundamentally that "of mental or spiritual anguish as the protagonist acts in the knowledge that what he must do is in some sense wrong—as he sees himself at once both good and bad, justified, yet unjustified." Finally, in the midst of all this, there emerges a perception of value. It is not so much that within the tragic framework suffering becomes redemptive nor that the tragic sufferer grows in the traditional virtues of love and loyalty. There is rather a moment of discovery of a higher level of being which remains closed to those who did not suffer in this way, be they the counselors of Job or the chorus surrounding Oedipus. Some hint about the truth of the human condition emerges.[5]

He insists that the term not be misconstrued as another diatribe against the institutional church or its leadership's abuses of authority. Rather, he considers seriously an aspect of ecclesial life and explores how this pain, suffering, and anger might challenge and enrich the self-understanding of the church. When placed in the context of the Second Vatican Council's recognition of the need for "continual reformation" (*UR,* 6) I can imagine no better appreciation of the ordeal-and-endurance of interchurch families than through McConville's development of this "tragic" component of "ecclesiadicy." He reminds us that the human, limited, finite and historical church is not synonymous with the kingdom of God, but ever striving to realize the eschatological coming of the new order of relationships among people. Interchurch families are integral to that process. Because they neither emigrate nor despair, "however bleak their experience of the ecclesial landscape may be," says McConville, victims of ecclesiadicy "look for places where they can together wait in hope for spring."[6]

We read more and more of that drama of interchurch families when celebrity occasions the telling of their story. Syndicated columnist Mary McGrory wrote a compelling testimony of Congressman Mickey Leland, murdered in Ethiopia while investigating reports of refugee food being diverted:

> Leland was an ardent ecumenist. He believed that Jews and blacks could get along well, and sent dozens of young blacks from the Houston ghetto to work in Israeli fields. He also firmly told their Israeli hosts that the Palestinians deserve a homeland.
>
> At the baptism of his adored son, Jarrett, now 3, Leland managed to persuade the authorities of the Roman Catholic Church, who can be stuffy about this

sort of thing, to allow Bishop Desmond Tutu to perform the service.[7]

Over fifteen years ago, the Anglican-Roman Catholic International Commission on the Theology of Marriage and Its Application to Mixed Marriages, and the dialogue among the Lutheran World Federation, the World Alliance of Reformed Churches, and the Roman Catholic Church both appealed for the dissolving of "canonical form" requirements by the Roman Catholic Church (which we examined in Chapter 2) to recognize the marriage contracted at a non-Roman Catholic church.[8] Our religious xenophobia appears destined for extinction because such unilateral demands can no longer be justified when the church has made irreversible ecumenical commitments. In McConville's terms, there is this *tragic* element to the church, perpetuating a violence of mistrust and fear, which is more subtle but even more damaging than physical violence.

The vectors for church unity have been plotted in the *koinonia* model of unity. But are Christian persons, indeed whole parishes and congregations, moving toward such a destination?

Patrick Granfield has remarked that, ecumenically speaking, the church is in a period of "consolidation." He identifies three separate stages in the development of the ecumenical movement, indeed in any society: creativity, consolidation, and formalism. We can expect none of the excitement, the newsworthy civil rights photography (or sound bytes) with rabbis and Protestant ministers and sisters in habits, along with Roman-collared priests marching arm in arm, scenes that typified the creative moment of the late 1960s. The enthusiasm to implement the ecumenical vision and change whatever was incompatible with it seems to have waned into a complacency with the clumsy status

quo. However, this is not to underestimate the power of consolidation periods. "In the period of consolidation," says
Granfield, "a more dispassionate assessment takes place.
The flush of creativity gives way to the hard work of making
firm the gains of the earlier period, of avoiding fragmenta-
tion and excess." He cautions against this consolidation
deteriorating into "the social paralysis" of formalism "with
its defensive and rigid stability." The temptation, in Granfield's surmise, is "to revert to an out-dated formalism" and
lapse into the defensiveness that had finally thawed in the
ecumenical movement's birth during the early decades of
the twentieth century.[9]

Walbert Bühlmann also has spoken in terms of "consolidation," "a certain quiet" settling upon the church in the
wake of the "stormy upheaval" during the conciliar and
post-conciliar period. His reading finds this inevitable period of "consolidation" less benign than in Granfield's interpretation. "Order and discipline within, decisiveness and
uniformity without—in the direction of 'enemies'—are to be
the important passwords now to be passed on and carried
through."[10] In effect, consolidation spells reactionary formalism for Bühlmann.

Perhaps it is important, in this regard, to return to Karl
Rahner and his vision of a courageous theological reflection
and pastoral ministry for the future church. When asked to
assess the Second Vatican Council and the time since then,
he responded that the council "has not really been put into
practice in the Church, either according to its letter or according to its spirit." Thus, for Rahner, "we are living
through a 'wintry season.'"[11] In 1984, shortly before his
death, when Rahner was pressed about the juridical, institutional and church-political "side questions" that eclipse the
central gospel issues, he voiced an irrepressible hope. "If
Christianity really possessed that degree of radical hope," he

said, "which by nature it demands, then it would be spring-time in the Church." This, in Rahner's words, involved the response to a personal challenge to bring to life the very "inner core of faith."[12] In these pages I have attempted to capture such a springtime of hope and faith radiating from the lives of truly interchurch families.

In May of 1987 I prepared a paper for the International Association of Interchurch Families Conference gathered in Lingfield, Surrey, England. As the first American to par-ticipate in this European biannual event, I had carefully chronicled the foundations of our "sister" association which would be born in the United States in January of 1988. I introduced my remarks[13] with the recollection of a question from one of my students. "What are you going to talk to them about?" she had prodded. I replied, in the buzz-words of the day, "It's ecumenism! You know, '*glasnost*' and '*peristroika*' for the church!"

Nowhere in contemporary ecumenical experience do "openness" and "restructuring" (though not of the *economic* variety) more immediately engage and challenge the churches than in the persons of interchurch family mem-bers. Theirs is a daily test of our ecumenical will and resolve. The past few years have witnessed some unimaginable events throughout Eastern Europe: election of a poet-phi-losopher to lead Czechoslovakia, the reunification of Ger-many, and the Soviet Union's transition to a free market economy. Above all, the collapse of the Berlin Wall as a sym-bol of the Cold War has reversed western political ideology and propaganda. What was once despised as the ugly epit-ome of repression and political tyranny has been trans-formed into symbolic chips of cinder block, prized trophies of liberation and new freedom. One is immediately tempted to imagine the ecumenical breakthrough coming with a sur-prising chain of similarly unpredictable and irrepressible events. What will we identify as the symbolic mementos, the relic-chips from "walls" of denominationalism that come tumbling down? The status quo of our political order changed precipitously, only because at the grassroots the time was ripe. The ecumenical status quo will ultimately change, not merely because of agreed statements and theological dialogues, but because the truth of these official conversations has been received in the lives and experiences of baptized Christians of diverse traditions. Can we imagine anyone more convincingly empowered than interchurch families to lead the churches in this reception of the *koinonia* vision of the future church?

The most frequent image of the ecumenical process is that of a pilgrimage—the very metaphor of our opening scenario, the interchurch family caravan at the crossroad. We know our destination, the restoration of full communion among the churches, Christians gathered for a celebration of the eucharist at a common table, sharing the one bread and the one cup as a sacrament of the risen Christ. The potential of a servant-church in mission to the world's suffering and damaged people finds its source, as we explored in Chapter 4, in the intellectual, moral, and religious conversions to which ecumenism invites us. Each intermediate point of the journey is, then, not diminished, but takes on added importance for pilgrims. It is their personal interaction, the confidences and trust that are exchanged in each day's narratives and presence with one another, that sustain the momentum toward the distant but ever-nearing goal. One requirement of any pilgrim is to leave something behind in order to venture forth into the future. Here the "paradigm shift" (explored in this book's sixth chapter) in our understanding of the church and the relationship of all baptized persons has challenged us to leave behind historic, but limited, concepts. New ways of perceiving, experiencing, and understanding, in turn, affect our ability to make judgments and decisions on the basis of the new paradigm. More specifically, the *koinonia* paradigm affords new possibilities for interchurch families and others to make visible our unity in the church's sacramental life by ways that the old models excluded.

The opening lines of the Second Vatican Council's Decree on Ecumenism spoke bluntly, identifying the restoration of Christian unity as "one of the principal concerns" of the council. The division of the churches "openly contradicts the will of Christ, scandalizes the world, and damages that most holy cause, the preaching of the gospel to every creature" (*UR* 1). The choice of the word *scandal* deliberately focused the ecumenical vision. Quite literally, the word means "obstacle," "a stumbling block." In this sense, the church as the *pilgrim* people of God (*LG* 14, 47–51) admits being impeded from progressing through interim steps toward the full communion Christ intends for all baptized Christians. Interchurch families remind us by their unity as family of our failure to make visible the unity we are called to manifest as churches.

Would it not be possible for the American Catholic bishops to continue the momentum of their constructive pastoral letters on peacemaking (*The Challenge of Peace,* 1983), and the national economy (*Economic Justice for All,* 1986) with a new pastoral letter on ecumenism? An apt analogy could be made to their argument on nuclear weapons, where the bishops insisted that a time would come when even possession of nuclear weapons as a "deterrent" could no longer be tolerated as an end in itself, because it can be tolerated only as a temporary step on the way to progressive disarmament. Here is an explicit claim of an expiration date on the deterrence theory.[14] This moral argument led to the conclusion that while unilateral disarmament may not be a clear moral mandate, unilateral steps toward multilateral disarmament certainly are. What if the bishops similarly concluded that the period for tolerating the morally evil "status quo" of lack of full communion with other Christians had likewise expired? What if the bishops served ecumenism by a positive, constructive endeavor, proactively implementing the unfulfilled ecclesiology of the Second Vatican Council, rather than reacting in terms of exceptional juridical indults (the nuclear deterrence approach to Christian unity)? What would this argument persuade them to propose as the next specific, visible steps toward the Roman Catholic Church's morally claimed goal of the restoration of full communion with other Christians? In interchurch families?

Karl Rahner proposed an honest humility for Roman Catholics who inflate various degrees of church teaching to the caliber of dogma, the church's authoritative interpretation and promulgation of revealed truth. A twofold concern emerged: (1) the need to make it possible for other Christians to recognize their faith in Catholic teaching; (2) the need to correct Roman Catholics' incorrect misunderstandings identified as dogma. "Our work consists, then, not only in enlightening non-Catholic Christians and theologians," Rahner cautioned, "but first of all enlightening ourselves, in purifying our own faith from misunderstandings that we ourselves continue to convey out of inertia or out of an exaggerated confidence in our own convictions."[15] How often in interchurch pastoral care is this principle of the "hierarchy of truths" (*UR,* 11) compromised? This book has illustrated how interchurch families move the church beyond both inertia and exaggeration.

Jean Caffey Lyles, senior news editor of *The Lutheran,* in a recent article for a Lilly Endowment report on mainline Protestant churches entitled "The Fading of Denomina-

tional Distinctiveness," signaled the importance of Robert
Wuthnow's "cutting edge" book, *The Restructuring of American Religion.* While the Princeton University researcher contends that it overstates the case to suggest that denominationalism no longer carries weight, he proceeds to correlate
switching denominations with college education and, in the
same breath, mentions that "intermarriage is often a strong
influence." Lyles also cites Wade Clark Roof and William
McKinney's work, *American Mainline Religion: Its Changing
Shape and Future,* for identifying the "new voluntarism" in
American culture. This inclination for "what serves individual needs," say these researchers, "takes preference over an
inherited tie to a particular denomination." The pick-and-choose or "cafeteria of options" trend for religious identity,
McKinney says, puts the future both of denominations and
the ecumenical movement "in serious trouble." The advantages accrue to individual congregations which tend, by
contrast, to be "much healthier." The paradox for mainline
churches lingers in the fact, observed by Wuthnow, that
more of his fellow Presbyterians "mingle with, marry the
members of, and switch to other denominations now than
ever before" because the growth of the ecumenical movement, culture diversity and tolerance have made easier such
denominational crossings. Lyles confirms this fact that inherited religious loyalties no longer guarantee denominational futures by quoting a 1980 Gallup survey that showed
fewer than half (43%) of adults in the United States had
always claimed the same religion or denomination, and at
least 40% of Protestants in this country have switched denominational affiliations.[16] One can conjecture that the majority of mixed marriages, as reported in the demographics
of our first chapter, distribute according to these trends that
trivialize ecumenism and denominational identity. Interchurch families, by contrast, promote a deeper ecumenism

that attracts persons to fidelity in their respective traditions, and at the same time empowers them to serve as midwives for the *koinonia* of separated churches.

The greatest natural allies for ecumenists advocating the gifts of interchurch families are Family Ministry professionals around the country. Most dioceses now subsidize this growing ministry that touches the lives of parishioners more directly than any other diocesan agency. Such collaboration, however, would recommend that ecumenists not invent entirely new structures to respond to the phenomenon of interchurch families, but make more ecumenically responsive the existing Family Ministry structures. Marriage preparation, Engaged Encounter, and Marriage Encounter programs already serve gatherings that, in many locales, number more "mixed marriage" couples than Catholic-Catholic partners.

Alasdair Heron suggested almost twenty years ago that the fact of interchurch marriage places two principles, which ordinarily are mutually supportive, into conflict: church membership and family. In other words, loyalty to each produces a new tension in interchurch families. Christian marriage intends to reinforce the "ecclesial character" of the family. But "church and marriage," concluded Heron, "which in principle belong together, have fallen out of phase with each other because of the division between the churches; and thus the identity of the church and the marriage alike is threatened," producing a "radical ecclesiological incoherence" for interchurch families.[17]

Dennis Guernsey,[18] an academician and Family Ministry practitioner, has made a similar analysis by remarking that the family historically proved the depository of primary relationships such as intimacy, personal development, and sensitivity; tasks performed by the family were secondary. With modern culture, Guernsey points out, the family becomes dysfunctional when secondary relationships such as functional, impersonal tasks of jobs, career, travel, and consumption push these primary relationships into a secondary category. This reversal means that in many families children and adults lose the ethos in which vulnerability, communication, personal relationships, affectivity, and expressiveness are naturally learned. When members of a family, children in particular, have no healthy primary relationships, they cannot relate meaningfully to God. I have suggested throughout this book that the dysfunction becomes scandalously compounded when the churches deny to baptized Christians (who ought to relate to one another as if they were a family of faith: "brothers and sisters in Christ") the recognition that the grace present in the ultimate primary human relationships of spouses, children, and parents is integral to their experience of the sacraments. Does this not suggest that the church itself must continue to be reformed when it evidences symptoms of being a dysfunctional family?

It is fitting to conclude this study with two auspicious signals of hope for interchurch families.

First, in February 1988 a plenary meeting of the Vatican's then Secretariat for Promoting Christian Unity received responses from national episcopal conferences on a draft of the new *Ecumenical Directory,* to update the two-part earlier edition of 1967 and 1970. Monsignor Eleuterio F. Fortino, undersecretary of the secretariat, has reported that attention to the evolving, organic process necessitates what Pope John Paul II described as "directives based on doctrine and yet corresponding to present-day problems as well as being open to future developments." Not only is the collaborative consultation for the directory an encouraging sign, but the inclusion of "intercommunion and mixed marriages" as one of four sections of the text indicates the rising consciousness of the gifts and needs of interchurch families.[19] Early drafts of the *Ecumenical Directory* were significant in at least two regards. First, the authors recognized that the other spouse has a religious freedom and conscience, and in some cases the children will not be baptized and brought up as Catholics. The Catholic spouse would not fall subject to any church censure, but would continue to be obliged to share faith in forms of spiritual ecumenism in the family, and word and example that best enable other family members to appreciate the specific values of the Catholic tradition. And, second, the drafters addressed the neuralgic issue of eucharistic sharing in light of the communion which already exists between spouses who share the sacrament of baptism and matrimony. The need of spiritual help to maintain marital unity, the participation of the other Christian parent in a child's catechetical formation, and the growing appreciation of the centrality of eucharist in responding to personal spiritual crises in marriage are all acknowledged as possibly indicating the spiritual need for eucharistic sharing. The tone and careful context of this section could move many bishops from previously rigorist interpretations of the canonical questions and clarify the confusion between intercommunion and eucharistic sharing which we examined in Chapter 3.

Second, in October 1989 the Joint Working Group of the Roman Catholic Church and the World Council of Churches sponsored a consultation on mixed marriages in Geneva.[20] In addition to assessing related developments in various bilateral dialogues and the growth in numbers of mixed marriages, the consultation drafted a report in which pastoral care of mixed marriages pressed new developments raised in the fourth and fifth chapters of this book. Eucharistic sharing received special attention with reference to the possibility of children being turned away from the faith because of their perplexity over communion rules and their need to receive communion with both parents together. But the consultors appealed to a recognition that we are in an evolutionary situation, an intermediate state which is bound to be anomalous as we progress toward the recovery of full communion. In a forthright discussion of baptismal discipline, the report acknowledges the developments in double belonging. Some couples, as we have already studied, have difficulty in choosing one church or another, and prefer to enrich the child with an experience of the life of both churches. The report goes so far as to promote, at least where the Roman Catholic Church is concerned, the minister or priest of the other church assisting at the baptism of an interchurch child, and the registration of the baptism in both churches if parents request. The consultation suggested that such double belonging can be even stronger in children of interchurch families.

Double belonging will undoubtedly emerge more and more as a concrete expression in interchurch family life and pastoral reflection. The 1990 recommended guidelines from the Southern Baptist–Roman Catholic pastoral dialogue in Louisville, Kentucky aptly addressed the challenge: "As churches, we listen intently to the prophetic witness of those families who live more fully a deeper belonging to both churches."[21] In English Anglican–Roman Catholic dialogue, the question of double belonging has been addressed with the helpful distinction between formal "membership" in a church and "belonging" in a less juridical sense.[22] The 1992 international Association of Interchurch Families (AIF) meeting in Dunblane, Scotland has chosen as its theme "Listen to Our Story," intending to emphasize double belonging in the experience and spirituality of interchurch children.[23]

Ecumenists, family ministers, and every pastoral minister share a special responsibility to both interchurch families and the churches' leadership. They help those in authority to see how their ministry and what is important in the life of interchurch families are consistent. Indeed, they help commission interchurch families whom the Spirit empowers to serve the present and future church. Yet the continuing obstacles are formidable. The seemingly untimely (given the indication of an imminent new Vatican *Ecumenical Directory*) Bishops' Conference of England and Wales' revised directory *Mixed Marriage* (April 30, 1990) flatly discredits double belonging.[24] And a symptom of similar denial of interchurch family viability by the structures of the institutional church was embedded in a 1989 questionnaire to seminary administrators from the National Catholic Education Association, asking how much of a concern (read, "problem") they considered the growing number of interfaith marriages to be for priesthood candidates' formation.

We signaled in Chapter 6 of this study that Edward Schillebeeckx's christological affirmation that the negative experiences of contrast, personified in those at the margins, can prove revelatory. Surely the witness of every truly interchurch family both clarifies and manifests the fullness of the reality of Christian marriage and family life. What their experience redefines for us is something foundational about the essence of the church, seeking to recover full communion. The grace experienced by interchurch families strives to articulate the mystery of Christ present among us, by renewing the symbolic actions of the church's sacraments.

> If living human beings are the fundamental symbol of God (*imago Dei*), then the place where human beings are dishonoured and oppressed, both in the depth of their own hearts and in an oppressive society, is at the same time the privileged place where religious experience be-

comes possible in a life style which seeks to give form to that symbol, to heal and restore it to itself: to express its deepest truth.[25]

Someone recently asked me: "Have the churches and denominations been divided all your life?" I could only think of a similar question and the answer that gifted musician Stevie Wonder once gave.

Somebody asked Stevie Wonder: "Have you been blind all your life?"

He answered, smilingly, "Not yet!"

The élan of interchurch families transposes this very dialogue with their own irrepressible hope:

Somebody asked an interchurch family: "Have the churches been divided all your life?"

They answered, smilingly, "Not yet!"

Notes

[1]Michael Jackson and David Butler, *Catholics and Methodists: The Work of the International Commissions, 1967–86* (Peterborough/London: Methodist Publishing House/Catholic Truth Society: 1988) 15–16.

[2]See *Truth and Community: Diversity and Its Limits in the Ecumenical Movement* (Grand Rapids: Eerdmans, 1988), especially Chapter 2, "Foundations for the Ecumenical Vision," 19–37.

[3]"Imagination and Passion in the Ecumenical Movement," *Ecumenical Trends* 18 (1989) 100.

[4]William McConville, "The Sinful, the Tragic and Ecclesiadicy," paper presented at The Catholic Theological Society of America meeting, June 9, 1989, St. Louis, p. 1 (emphasis mine). He defines *ecclesiadicy:* "By it I mean simply this: speech or discourse about the church which attends in a special way to the sinful or tragic dimensions of the church, and the suffering which has thereby ensued, and seeks to reflect on the reality of the church in

face of this suffering" (10). Cf. "Seminar on Ecclesiology," CTSA *Proceedings* 44 (1989) 145–46.

⁵Ibid. 5–6.

⁶Ibid. 12.

⁷"A Man Who Cared," *The Courier-Journal,* August 17, 1989, A9.

⁸See Anglican–Roman Catholic International Commission, "Theology of Marriage and Its Application to Mixed Marriages," *Information Service* 32 (1976) 12–27, especially paragraphs 7 and 62, which called for the relaxation of canonical form; and Lutheran World Federation, World Alliance of Reformed Churches, Roman Catholic Church Dialogue, *Final Report: Theology of Marriage and the Problems of Mixed Marriage* (Washington, DC: United States Catholic Conference, 1978) 38–39. A recent review of interchurch marriage literature in the past fifteen years is Peter Hocken, "Covenants for Unity (3): Interchurch Marriages," *One in Christ* 25 (1989) 273–80. See also Leo C. Hay, *Eucharist: A Thanksgiving Celebration* (Wilmington: Michael Glazier, 1989) for a careful treatment of interchurch marriage in the context of his study of the eucharist.

⁹Patrick R. Granfield, "Ecclesiological Reflections," *Whither the Wind: A Telltale of Authority* (Dover: EDEO–NADEO, 1987) 45–46. Martin Reardon identifies similar phases of ecumenism with the "ecumenical enthusiasts" in the thirty years prior to the Second World War; and the passing of initiative to leaders of the institutional churches for reforms (e.g. Councils of Churches, the Second Vatican Council). The British ecumenical process begun in 1982, "Not Strangers, but Pilgrims," eventuated in the 1987 Swanwick conference (England, Ireland, Scotland and Wales); its transition, "from cooperation to commitment," was formally covenanted in "Churches Together . . ." celebrations during October 1990. In effect, the British ecumenical process has succeeded in circumventing the formalism Granfield cautions against. See Martin Reardon, "English AIF Founder Visits U.S. Families," *The ARK* 2: 1 (April 1990) [Newsletter of the American Association of Interchurch Families] 1–2.

[10]Walbert Buhlmann, "Preface," *The Church of the Future: A Model for the Year 2001* (Maryknoll: Orbis, 1986) xi–xii.

[11]Karl Rahner, *Faith in a Wintry Season: Conversations and Interviews with Karl Rahner in the Last Years of His Life* (New York: Crossroad, 1990) 39.

[12]Ibid. 200.

[13]George Kilcourse, "U.S. Interchurch Families: Ecumenism with a Human Face," *One in Christ* 24 (1988) 243–51.

[14]*The Challenge of Peace: God's Promise and Our Response* (Washington, DC: United States Catholic Conference, 1983), nn. 173, 175–76, 188, 190. The bishops root their affirmation: "Each proposed addition to our strategic system or change in strategic doctrine must be assessed precisely in light of whether it will render steps toward 'progressive disarmament' more or less likely" (n. 188), in Pope John Paul II's 1982 Special Address to the United Nations. There the pope had declared, "In current conditions 'deterrence' based on balance, certainly not as an end in itself but as a step on the way toward a progressive disarmament, may still be judged morally acceptable." For a critique of *The Challenge of Peace* which I have applied analogously to interchurch marriage pastoral proposals, see Richard A. McCormick, "Nuclear Deterrence and the Problem of Intention: A Review of the Positions," *Catholics and Nuclear War: A Commentary on 'The Challenge of Peace,'* ed. P. Murnion (New York: Crossroad, 1983).

[15]Karl Rahner, "Open Questions in Dogma Considered by the Institutional Church as Definitively Answered," *Journal of Ecumenical Studies* 15 (1978) 211–26.

[16]Jean Caffey Lyles, "The Fading of Denominational Distinctiveness," *Progressions* 2:1 (January 1990) 16–17.

[17]Alasdair Heron, "The Ecclesiological Problems of Interchurch Marriage," *Beyond Tolerance,* ed. Michael Hurley (London: Geoffrey Chapman, 1975) 75–78.

[18]See Dennis Guernsey's *A New Design for Family Ministry* (Elgin: D.C. Cook, 1982); *The Family Covenant: Student's Manual* (Elgin: D.C. Cook, 1984); co-author with Ray S. Anderson, *On*

Being Family: A Social Theology of the Family (Grand Rapids: Eerdmans, 1985); co-author with Lucy G. Guernsey, *Real-Life Marriage* (Waco: Word Books, 1987).

[19]Eleuterio F. Fortino, "An Ecumenical Directory for a New Era," *Information Service* 67 (1988) 69–70.

[20]Cf. "Explorations and Responses: The Joint Working Group—Instrument of Dissent and Metanoia: A Discussion of the Issue of Mixed Marriage," *Journal of Ecumenical Studies* 23 (1986) 107–12.

[21]"Southern Baptist–Roman Catholic Interchurch Marriage Guidelines Recommended for The Archdiocese of Louisville and The Long Run Baptist Association," *Mid-Stream* 29 (1990) 303–12.

[22]W. Smith, unpublished paper, "Double Belonging," March 1, 1990.

[23]See Tim and Chantal Evans, "Thoughts on Interchurch Spirituality," *Interchurch Families* 20 (Winter 1988/9) 1–2.

[24]See, for example, *Mixed Marriage: The Revised Directory Promulgated by the Bishops' Conference of England and Wales, 30th April 1990* (London: The Incorporated Catholic Truth Society, 1990): "[I]t has been known, although very rarely, for Catholics to suggest that their children be both Catholics and also belong to the denomination of their partner. This is not possible" (15–16). The subsequent "theological reason" to support that claim makes no reference to the *koinonia* ecclesiology, which is the center of ARCIC dialogues officially sponsored by the Anglican and Roman Catholic churches as well as the official teaching of the two communions.

[25]Edward Schillebeeckx, "The Role of History in What Is Called the New Paradigm," *Paradigm Change in Theology,* ed. Hans Küng and David Tracy (New York: Crossroad, 1989) 318–19.

Appendix: A Dream About the Interchurch Future

Minutes of the Ecumenical Commission
(Diocese of Mainstream, U.S.A.—November 31, 1999)

The ecumenical commission met at 2:30 p.m. in the parish center of Blessed Thea Bowman Church: (I) to review final arrangements for the Week of Prayer for Christian Unity celebrations, January 18–25, 2000; and (II) to discuss reports on ongoing interchurch projects; and (III) to raise items of new business.

(I) Week of Prayer for Christian Unity Celebrations

(A) *LARC Covenant.* Sister Mildred Kildown, administrator of St. Theresa Parish, announced that the bishop would be celebrating eucharist on Sunday at their parish, with officially approved "interim eucharistic sharing" (according to the November 15, 1997 NCCB policy statement) for all visitors from the neighboring Episcopal and Lutheran churches. These three churches will be celebrating the 30th anniversary of their Lutheran/Anglican/Roman Catholic covenant. She reported that she has also been approached by some 75 interchurch couples from Methodist–, Disci-

167

ples–, and Presbyterian–Roman Catholic marriages, and that permission for "eucharistic sharing" had been appropriately extended.

(B) *Confirmations.* Mr. Peters, liturgical consultant for the Lutheran Synod, reported that the confirmations scheduled for that same Sunday would be celebrated at the 11 o'clock morning liturgy at the Episcopal cathedral—to avoid an afternoon schedule conflict with the Super Bowl Sunday broadcast. The final arrangements included each of the five bishops (Roman Catholic, Episcopal, United Methodist, Antiochian Orthodox, and Evangelical Lutheran Church in America) sitting in the sanctuary and confirming the candidates of the bishop's tradition as they approach. Special permission from the Orthodox ecumenical patriarchate has provided for the Roman Catholic bishop to preside at eucharist, and for "eucharistic sharing" opportunities to be extended to the families and guests of all the confirmation candidates. The confirmed will gather in interchurch teams after communion, to be missioned by bishops and catechists for their ministries with residents of the home of The Little Sisters of the Poor, and the Lutheran World Federation hunger and well-digging projects in Ethiopia. Grants for five of the newly confirmed to visit Ethiopia for six month internships are being funded by sale of third world crafts in six neighborhood churches during Advent.

(II) Reports: Ongoing Interchurch Projects

(A) *New Joint Parish.* Canon Butler of the Episcopal Diocese reported that the architect's designs had been released to contractors for bids on the new joint parish of Venerable Desmond Tutu Church in the eastern part of the county. The Episcopal and Roman Catholic bishops had met with attorneys to endorse their approval of the jointly-founded community. It is expected that their first celebrations will be on the first Sunday of Advent, 2002. The zoning commission has awarded a certificate of excellence to the architects for the project, in light of the space utilization factors in this crowded growth area. The ecological design of the building, its fuel efficiency and solar energy capacity, housing of a neighborhood health clinic, and the multipurpose education center are featured in the current issue of the magazine, *Church Architects.*

(B) *Interchurch Catechumenate.* Mrs. Margot Potter, of Midlands Evangelical Reformed Church, reported that the third year's "pilot" of a jointly sponsored catechumenate program with Roman Catholic, Lutheran, Disciples of Christ, Evangelical Reformed, and Southern Baptist candidates in the Oakwood suburb has attracted a total of 112 candidates, about equally distributed among the five participating churches. Speakers from each tradition have been recruited to deal with the specific catechetical topics in the weekly program. Competence and expertise are the only criteria for each of the speakers, who are invited by a joint planning committee. Topics include scripture, discipleship, worship, ethics, and understandings of the church. The RCIA task force in the diocese is consulting with Mrs. Potter to explore the possibility of a city-wide implementation of this model for a joint catechumenate program in other clusters of parishes and neighboring churches.

(C) *Interchurch Marriage Preparation.* The Presbyterian Church's executive has corresponded with the ecumenical commission's director and affirmed the local Presbytery's joint presentations in the Family Ministry's diocesan Marriage Preparation program: this brings to a total of eight the number of bilateral teams that are allotted one hour in the interchurch segment to orient and discuss with interchurch couples participating in the Roman Catholic Diocese's Marriage Preparation sessions each month. (The Episcopal

Diocese, the Southern Baptist local Association, United Methodist Diocese, Disciples of Christ Regional Area, Evangelical Lutheran Church in America Synod, Evangelical Reformed Church Assembly, and the United Church of Christ Council all already collaborate in the Family Ministry's program.) The Presbytery will also provide pastoral staff for the six month and eighteen month follow-up workshops for Presbyterian–Roman Catholic newly married couples. This brings to five the total number of bilateral follow-up programs in the diocese.

(D) *Interchurch L'Arche and AIDS Ministries.* (1) A cluster of five congregations in the downtown north side reported recently that they have now built a fifth residence for the l'Arche community of physically and mentally challenged young adults. The purpose is to promote the adult independence and community interdependence of these persons in ecumenical, small-group-living homes. The project began seven years ago by a dozen interchurch families from four of the congregations; it was evangelized by each of them in their churches and they soon recruited personnel and raised contributions for the first four houses. High school students from three schools now volunteer service in the l'Arche communities. Job opportunities for l'Arche participants now earn 25% of the operating costs of the properties, with projections that this will reach 50% in the next three years. (2) The southwest interchurch couples group is also in the second year of coordinating services, centered on meal deliveries for AIDS patients in their neighborhoods. They report particular interest and volunteerism by retired persons who offer their services in the kitchen (with home recipes) and in daily telephoning to persons with AIDS. A $400,000 United Way grant for 1999 (renewed for a fifth year) helped fund the fleet of vans and rental of two buildings used as kitchens and dining rooms.

(E) *Metropolitan Baptismal Records Database.* Miss Carol Allison of the chancery attended the meeting to advise us that the computerization of baptismal records by all the churches in the metropolitan area has been completed. She applauded the collaboration of the various judicatory heads in promoting this two year networking of computer systems. She noted the special cooperation of local independent churches in joining the network. It not only facilitates record-keeping, but in the case of interchurch families and engaged interchurch couples it provides easy access to baptismal certificates, which are produced on a common form. The National Council of Churches recently awarded Miss Allison its distinguished achievement award at its October meeting in Cleveland. The computer project is the first such in the nation, singled out by the NCC as a "visionary effort to anticipate the restoration of full communion by our churches, a visible and powerful contemporary sign of the unity we share in Christ." A spin-off of the project will be proceeds from copyrighting the computer programming for this database. Ron and Nancy Lazarus, an interchurch couple whose company contributed services in developing the program, estimate that applications for other metropolitan church uses will prompt $6,000 in sales over the next six months. Proceeds will be split between the publication fund of the local chapter of the American Association of Interchurch Families (AAIF) and the State Interchurch Committee for Alternatives to Capital Punishment.

(F) *Interchurch Deacon-Families.* Finally, Deacon Chris Anderson offered a brief report of the diocesan task force on interchurch families with deacons. Demographics, she said, indicate that now Roman Catholic and mainline Protestant churches have identified some 5000 couples in the United States whose families include interchurch spouses, one of whom (and sometimes both!) are deacons in the churches.

At their first convention scheduled for December 28, 1999 in Milwaukee, four seminars will address:

—how to edit your deacon-spouse's homilies;
—preparing the catechumenate notes for your spouse's classes;
—pre-marriage preparation for interchurch engaged couples;
—joint baptismal celebrations for infants in interchurch families.

Chris brought the commission up-to-date on plans by the bishops of the province to establish a joint diaconate preparation with corresponding Episcopal dioceses. Since many classes were conducted by the same college and seminary professors (previously at different sites) a joint task force has analyzed the content and curriculum of each church's program and concluded that 90% of the course can be jointly administered. (The joint Episcopal–Roman Catholic retreat for deacons and spouses last May occasioned a letter with 248 signatures recommending this development.)

(G) *Cathedrals' Easter Vigil.* Jamie and Michael Chance, an interchurch couple, reported that the thirty-five year old covenant between our Roman Catholic cathedral and the Episcopal cathedral will be marked with a joint Easter vigil liturgy in the Civic Plaza, midway (and a short walking distance) between both locations. A parade permit has been secured and city officials advised of the publicity surrounding the event. The two bishops will gather the communities for (1) a common liturgy of the word; (2) a common lighting of the Easter fire; and (3) a common pool for baptism of candidates, followed by their confirmation by their respective bishop. Separate eucharists would follow at the two cathedrals, thereby marking the scandal of the churches' continuing division on the feast of Easter.

(III) New Business

(A) *Joint NCCB/House of Bishops Meeting.* Bishop Martin Moore has written the commission to report on the favorable USCC action to sponsor a joint meeting of the National Conference of Catholic Bishops and the House of Bishops of the Episcopal Church in the U.S. The agenda includes a wide range of ecumenical concerns, particularly the recommendations of the Final Report of ARCIC II from 1998. Interchurch family ministry was identified as their second priority, with AAIF's Executive Committee having been invited by the joint planning team for the bishops to draft a proposed set of national Episcopal–Roman Catholic interchurch family guidelines. Top priority for the meeting will be a discussion of stewardship, with specific attention to federal and state grants to convert vacant church properties to low-cost housing and to staff geriatric day-care centers.

(B) *Ecumenical Council.* The bishop also reported that Pope John XXIV has asked for the Theological Commission of the forthcoming ecumenical council (to convene in his native city of Nairobi, Kenya on Pentecost Sunday, 2001) to prepare a report on the process to include designated theologians and bishops from our sister churches with full speaking and voting rights on the floor of the council. Particular concern for an intercultural dimension, to guarantee a voice for European and North American white minorities at the council, prompted his intervention.

(C) *The State Council of Churches' "Witness for Human Life."* Since last January's meeting of the judicatory heads of churches in the state, a task force has begun to implement their signed agreement that interchurch cooperation be more visible in the areas of opposition to capital punishment, as well as advocacy of ecological, geriatric, and unborn life issues. (1) During the summer an interchurch families' Teen Team committed itself to coordinate high school recycling education. They will launch a march across the state during spring-break week, building on the theme of "The earth is God's creation." Teen leaders will meet with committee chairs in the legislature to make specific recommendations for legislative incentives promoting mass transit systems, recycling centers, and wetlands/forest protection. (2) The State Council's Commission on Christian Unity began its third year of dialogue on "methods" of ethical decision-making among the various traditions. While they have agreed not to advocate any particular policy positions, they report they are nearing completion of an ethics "agenda" for the respective churches to assess.

(D) *AAIF Booths.* The Communications Committee of the local chapter of the American Association of Interchurch Families (AAIF) reports that booths used in the "pilot" exhibits at shopping malls throughout the city last January will be utilized in spring semester Family Fairs at area public high schools. Interchurch teens and couples will be able to present literature and videos about AAIF to students. It is expected to provide a contact with 12,500 area teens who are prospective interchurch couples. (Preliminary data from the U.S. Census bureau's 2000 project estimates that 63% of Americans between the ages of 18 and 34 are marrying a person outside their own religious tradition.)

(E) *International AIF.* Jim and Jenny Shuremount reported on the AAIF Executive Committee's planning for the 12th International Association of Interchurch Families conference, to convene in Arlington, Virginia, May 24–27, 2002. This first of the AIF conventions in the United States will welcome some 1,500 international delegates. The announced theme will be "A Third Generation: Children in Interchurch Families." Ten representatives from the local chapter are planning to participate, including four local children. Jim and Jenny's daughter, Corey, has been invited to lead a panel discussion on interchurch teen spirituality.

Because of the lengthy agenda surrounding The Week of Prayer for Christian Unity events, the commission agreed to distribute written reports from the Jewish-Catholic and Trialogue (Islamic-Catholic-Jewish) committees, and adjourned at 4:45 p.m. The next meeting will be on February 5 at 2:30 p.m. The meeting's agenda will begin with the two reports that were distributed at the November 31 session.

Index